Praise for *Jazz with*

"Writers and critics too often place music in style cubicles, partitioned off from the sounds around them. Only trouble is, artists rarely work that way. They have an open floor plan, and they mingle constantly. Tad Richards reaffirms that truth with a welcome dive into the under-explored and under-appreciated small swing combos and artists of the '40s and '50s, who made music from bebop to rhythm and blues. Richards finishes the book with a suggested soundtrack, which clinches his argument that if these artists are sometimes tough to categorize, they're always a pleasure to hear."

— David Hinckley, former pop culture
columnist, *New York Daily News*

"This is one of those books that we—jazz critics, jazz historians, jazz audiences, jazz musicians—have long needed. For a long time, these kinds of musical offshoots of jazz have been consigned by jazz people to mere footnotes in music history, but for the musicians who played this hybrid music called, in many cases, rhythm and blues, it was a living and it was life at a different, alternative, musical level. For audiences it was dance and fun and, later, nostalgia, a way of reliving the days when black popular music was a social thing in a much different way than 'modern' jazz was, for audiences of all colors and backgrounds. It is not that this kind of music has not been written about, but that few authors have had enough of a jazz background to fully understand the form and the context, as an offshoot of improvised music that was very rooted, not only in the black community, but in a concept of black entertainment that extended back to the early part of the twentieth century. It is well-researched and well-written, a rare book that shows both musical and social understanding and never sacrifices one for the other."

— Allen Lowe, musician and author of
*Turn Me Loose White Man: Or: Appropriating Culture:
How to Listen to American Music 1900–1960* and
That Devilin' Tune: A Jazz History, 1900–1950

Jazz with a Beat

Jazz with a Beat

Small Group Swing, 1940–1960

TAD RICHARDS

**EXCELSIOR
EDITIONS**

Cover: Portrait of Illinois Jacques by Tad Richards.

Published by State University of New York Press, Albany

© 2024 State University of New York

Excelsior Editions is an imprint of State University of New York Press

For information, contact State University of New York Press, Albany, NY
www.sunypress.edu

Library of Congress Cataloging-in-Publication Data

Name: Richards, Tad, author.
Title: Jazz with a beat : small group swing, 1940–1960 / Tad Richards.
Description: Albany : State University of New York Press, [2024]. | Series:
    Excelsior editions | Includes bibliographical references and index.
Identifiers: LCCN 2023019236 | ISBN 9781438496016 (hardcover : alk. paper) |
    ISBN 9781438496023 (ebook) | ISBN 9781438496009 (pbk. : alk. paper)
Subjects: LCSH: Swing (Music)—History and criticism. | Jazz—History and
    criticism.
Classification: LCC ML3508 .R53 2023 | DDC 781.650973—dc23/eng/20230523
LC record available at https://lccn.loc.gov/2023019236

10 9 8 7 6 5 4 3 2 1

To the memory of Wendell Jones.
He and I discovered this music together, as young teenagers,
and fell under its spell. He left us way too soon,
in 1964 at age twenty-one, but his memory inhabits every note.

I feel that these guys in this era made a greater contribution than they are recognized for.

—Joe Liggins

Contents

Illustrations

Introduction

The 1950s were a remarkably robust era for jazz. Benny Goodman, Louis Armstrong, and Dizzy Gillespie were all anointed by the US State Department as goodwill ambassadors, bringing the sound of America to the world. Goodman jammed with the clarinet-playing king of Thailand, and Dave Brubeck, although not sponsored by the State Department, brought jazz behind the Iron Curtain. Early in the decade, Brubeck had brought jazz to college, opening up a vast new market, and as it drew to a close, he recorded the first million-selling jazz album, *Time Out*, in 1959. In that same year, Miles Davis recorded *Kind of Blue*, which would become the top-selling jazz album of all time.

Jazz was on television. Steve Allen's popular late-night and primetime shows frequently featured jazz artists (Allen himself was an accomplished jazz pianist); *Stars of Jazz* had a three-year run and won an Emmy; and a private eye show, *Peter Gunn*, which used a jazz theme and regularly featured scenes with a jazz club as a backdrop, became so popular that soon jazz was the music that cued TV suspense, danger, or romance with sexual overtones. The movies also embraced jazz. Film composer Elmer Bernstein used a jazz motif for his score for *The Man with the Golden Arm* (1956). *Peter Gunn* made Henry Mancini one of Hollywood's most sought-after composers. Recognized jazz masters like Duke Ellington and John Lewis were commissioned to write scores for big-budget films.

Jazz festivals, most prominently the Newport Jazz Festival, were a new cultural phenomenon, with a documentary about the 1958 festival, *Jazz on a Summer's Day*, becoming a surprise hit. And the leading influencer of the day (although that term was still more than half a century away from popularity), *Playboy* magazine, began an annual jazz poll.

But then things changed. A gauntlet was thrown down by an album released on Atlantic Records in 1959: *The Shape of Jazz to Come* by Ornette

1

Coleman; it could not be ignored. Coleman was the most controversial, polarizing figure to come along in a long time. He was hailed, he was hated. Most of all, he was talked about. His music acquired the label of "free jazz"; others were playing it, most notably one of the most popular instrumentalists of the late '50s, John Coltrane. New stars in the free jazz firmament included Eric Dolphy, Albert Ayler, and Pharoah Sanders. The floodgates were open. But only a tiny percentage of the public was following. For many listeners, it was too weird, too experimental, too cacophonous.

At the same time, rock 'n' roll, dismissed as music for half-educated teenagers in the 1950s, became rock, a cultural phenomenon. The *Playboy* Jazz Poll became the *Playboy* Jazz and Pop poll, and Paul McCartney replaced Paul Chambers as a perennial poll winner.

But not every young jazz musician followed Ornette Coleman's siren song. Another new school of jazz was forming. Ray Charles had shown the way, and young musicians like Horace Silver and Jimmy Smith followed: jazz that was funkier, more immediate, more visceral, more danceable—"soul jazz."

The two schools coexisted within the pages of *DownBeat* and other periodicals that had begun to take jazz seriously as an art form. Jimmy Smith was as likely to get a five-star *DownBeat* review as Eric Dolphy. Soul jazz was a real thing, a niche music, but with a solid base of popularity—in the record stores, in the clubs, in colleges, in the Black communities, and also in the jazz media. Jazz had bifurcated and had done so successfully. It was a new phenomenon.

Except that it wasn't. *The exact same thing* had happened two decades earlier, and it was barely noticed. A second, more easily graspable genre of jazz developed alongside the more critically heralded bebop.

The received wisdom about jazz is this: it was "America's popular music" in the 1930s, but its popularity was dashed by the rise of the cerebral, undanceable bebop music of Charlie Parker, Dizzy Gillespie, and the other modernists. It became forever a niche music, never to achieve that popularity again. This is false for a couple of significant reasons.

First, jazz was always a niche music. The 1930s saw a surge in popularity of dance bands led by white bandleaders. Some of them, like Artie Shaw and Benny Goodman, were playing jazz, or "hot" music, as it was called at the time.[1] Some bands, notably Glen Gray's Casa Loma Orchestra, employed brilliant white jazz soloists like Bix Beiderbecke and Frankie Trumbauer, but their charts were primarily "sweet" music for society dancing. Others, most notably the Glenn Miller Orchestra, which was immensely popular, are included when people talk about the popular heyday of jazz, but while Miller made an enduring contribution to American music, it wasn't exactly jazz. Granted, this can be argued. There's no one definition of jazz that fits all contenders, and I don't propose to argue every borderline case. I would put Jimmy Dorsey into the hot category and Tommy Dorsey into the sweet, and Tommy might well have agreed with me. When the brothers split in 1935 and Tommy formed his own band, he was more or less under orders from his management to cut out the hot stuff. Bing Crosby had been an early pioneer of jazz singing, the first white singer to absorb the lessons of Louis Armstrong, but by the mid-1930s he had overtaken Rudy Vallee to become the premiere crooner of sweet ballads. I'm not going to haggle over exactly what the line is between hot and sweet music; I'll simply say that it was white dance bands, and not jazz, that dominated American music in the 1930s.

But the Black bands who had developed the music, whose pioneering work Goodman and Shaw and Beiderbecke had built on (Goodman hired Fletcher Henderson behind the scenes as an arranger; Don Redman wrote arrangements for Jimmy Dorsey and Harry James), remained a niche market, booked into Black venues, their records mostly marketed to and bought by Blacks. A look at the *Billboard* charts for the late 1930s verifies this. 1936 saw one record by a Black jazzman, Fats Waller's "It's a Sin to Tell a Lie." Benny Goodman was popular, and Tommy Dorsey's jazz combo, the Clambake Seven, had one hit, but for the most part the list is dominated by Eddy Duchin, Guy Lombardo, the sweet Tommy Dorsey, and the like. Waller had another hit in 1937, as did Duke Ellington; and Teddy Wilson, gaining fame as Benny Goodman's piano player, had two, with vocals by Billie Holiday.

While 1938 saw Chick Webb top the charts, largely due to his amazing new vocalist, Ella Fitzgerald, and her irresistible novelty record, "A-Tisket, A-Tasket," there was little else by Black musicians (Duke Ellington and Andy Kirk were the others). 1939 was all white, and almost all Glenn Miller (six of the top 12 tunes for the year); Benny Goodman and Artie Shaw had one top 20 hit each, and Glen Gray's Casa Loma Orchestra had two. The rest were dance bands with only the most tangential relation to jazz.

And this didn't change much in the 1940s. Hitmakers in 1941 were Glenn Miller, Freddy Martin, the Dorseys, and Horace Heidt. The years 1942–44 were anomalies, because the production of records was brought to a standstill by a strike against the record labels called by James C. Petrillo, the autocratic head of the American Federation of Musicians.

The companies could only release recordings hurriedly made before the strike date. As a result, no new acts were introduced. The product output was thin, but the names were the same, as was the melanin content of the musicians.

So throughout this era, jazz was a niche music, not "America's popular music," although some white jazz musicians like Goodman and Shaw were able to ride the bandwagon of swing. That didn't really change in the 1940s, although the emphasis switched from bandleader-as-star to vocalist-as-star, partly due to the changing economics of the era, partly to the musicians' strike which did not affect vocalists, and partly to the soaring popularity of Frank Sinatra.

But jazz changed. It changed quickly, and it changed dramatically. Some say it changed with one solo—Charlie Parker's improvisation in the Jay McShann orchestra's 1942 recording of "Sepian Bounce." McShann played classic Kansas City swing, but Parker's solo took that bluesy, danceable style, just for the space of one solo, in a whole new direction. The camel's nose was under the tent, and anywhere there was a jukebox, young musicians exhausted their supply of nickels listening to it. Parker's improvisations on "Cherokee," in the McShann band's live performances, were similarly galvanizing a new generation of musicians, and the chords to "Cherokee" would not long after become the basis for Parker's bebop tour de force "Ko-Ko."

And curiously, at right around this same time, the swing era was being attacked from another direction. In 1940, sportswriter-actor-jazz buff Heywood Hale Broun went from New York to New Orleans and recorded a group of old-time jazzmen led by trumpeter Henry "Kid" Rena (pronounced Renay). This was the beginning of the rediscovery of the traditional New Orleans sound that had gone out of fashion, eclipsed by swing, dismissed as old hat. To the new champions of New Orleans–style music, it was the only real jazz. Swing was diluted, cheesy, fake. And within a few years, the bebop partisans were rejecting swing as old hat. The jazz wars were on in earnest, with poor old swing battered from both sides.

But there are a few things to keep in mind here. First, swing did not exactly curl up and die. It still had its fans, and they were still a healthy percentage of music lovers. The "real jazz" traditionalists were a cult. They were right about the importance of a music that should not have been forgotten, and they performed a valuable service, but they were never more than a small segment of the music-consuming public. The bebop partisans were the avant garde, and the avant garde is, by definition, ahead of the curve: a small, self-selected group.

So what was jazz? This was a question no one had thought to ask, let alone answer, until the "real jazz" traditionalists came up with an answer that satisfied no one but themselves. But it was a start. And in order to rebut them, it was necessary to come up with a more inclusive definition. But, as it turned out, not much more inclusive.

Jazz was inexorably changed by Parker and the other young musicians who created the new music that came to be known as bebop, and it was changed in more ways than one. The music made stringent demands on the listener's attention. It valued individual expression and virtuosity over a danceable groove. And it was made by musicians who consciously rejected the vaudevillian, dance-hall showmanship that had characterized Black music and musicians of the past. But not all jazz musicians, and not all Black audiences, were ready to follow the thorny trail to bebop.

Swing music, especially the big band swing music of the 1930s, had mostly run its course, as all musical styles do. Audiences had changed. The Depression was winding down. President Franklin D. Roosevelt's Lend-Lease Program, followed by the United States' entry into the conflict that soon came to be known as World War II, meant a dramatic upturn in manufacturing and new job openings that extended even to the minority communities traditionally hardest hit by a shrinkage in the labor market. There was a new audience looking for a new sound, and musicians were ready to give it to them.

Charlie Parker was twenty-two when he recorded "Sepian Bounce" in 1942, and that same year a nineteen-year-old jazz musician, Illinois Jacquet, hired the year before by Lionel Hampton, was tapped by his boss to play the solo on a new recording of "Flying Home," a tune written by Hampton and Goodman and originally recorded by Goodman's sextet. That recording had featured a memorable solo by guitarist Charlie Christian, so it was known to be a reputation-maker.

Jacquet played his first solo in a Lester Young style, then decided that for his second solo, he wanted to do something really different. Improvising on the fly, he started with a strongly emphasized note, then played the same note again, then again. How long could he keep it up? Nine more times, the same note, then a little coda, then back to it again, again the same note repeated twelve times, before picking up the melody again. The effect on listeners in 1942 was electrifying, but more immediately,

Jacquet had electrified his bandmates. There's a heightened excitement when the ensemble swings back into action, and the recording climaxes with Hampton and trumpeter Ernie Royal trading single notes to keep that excitement going.

Also in 1942, a group called Louis Jordan and His Tympany Five had their first hit records on *Billboard*'s Harlem Hit Parade chart. "I'm Gonna Leave You on the Outskirts of Town" went to number three, and it was followed with his first number one, "What's the Use of Getting Sober (When You're Gonna Get Drunk Again)." Jordan, an alto sax player and vocalist, had been with the Chick Webb Orchestra; when he started his own group (although he called them the Tympany Five, there were rarely exactly five members), he hoped to recreate the sound and the feeling of Chick Webb's ensemble with a small group. Jordan would go on to have one of the most popular Black groups of the 1940s.

So 1942 is as good a place as any to mark the beginning of this new music that was growing up, unheralded, alongside the controversial but publicized sound of bebop: the big band jazz of the 1930s being reconfigured and rearranged for the more flexible small groups of the 1940s, a new breed of soloists pushing the sound of swing in a more contemporary direction. But was the music they were playing jazz?

There's no one definition of jazz. The New Orleans traditionalists' "real jazz" hung on as late as 1962, when Samuel B. Charters and Leonard Kunstadt, in their book *Jazz: A History of the New York Scene*, make a distinction between swing and jazz. Louis Armstrong dismissed Dizzy Gillespie and the beboppers as "poor little cats who have lost their way," and Cab Calloway denounced the sound as "Chinese music." Later, Miles Davis would describe Ornette Coleman as "all screwed up inside." And it's hard to imagine anyone from an earlier era finding much common ground with Vijay Iyer. Probably the best definition of jazz is the least helpful, from an academic's perspective. It comes from Louis Armstrong: "If you have to ask what jazz is, you'll never know."

So I'm not going to argue the case, I'm just going to state it. This music, made by Black musicians for Black audiences beginning in the early 1940s, parallel to bebop, sometimes crossing paths with it, sometimes diverging, was jazz. But as "jazz" was being defined in this era, and during this period of competing definitions, one new genre of jazz found itself getting left out of every definition.

Strangely, the modernists and the traditionalists were more united than they themselves realized at the time. The traditionalists despised swing as a dilution of the real thing, watered down, smoothed out, its African American roots corrupted by saccharine Tin Pan Alley songs, pandering to the masses. The modernists saw themselves in the vanguard of a new art form, a music that was to be taken seriously as Art with a capital A, not one that pandered to the masses.

Gradually, an umbrella definition began to emerge. Real jazz was authentic. It was real because it was artistically pure, like bebop. It was real because it had authentic roots, like New Orleans jazz. Or it was real because it just was, because it was played by masters like Louis Armstrong, Count Basie, Duke Ellington, Benny Goodman, or Bix Beiderbecke. Pallid imitators like Artie Shaw or Glenn Miller were out (although Shaw has certainly since been let back in). It was real because authorities recognized by *Metronome* editors Leonard Feather and Barry Ulanov, both of whom would write highly regarded books on the subject, certified it as real.

One panel of authorities was assembled by Feather and Belgian jazz critic Robert Goffin, out of dissatisfaction with the philistinism of the readers' polls in *DownBeat* and *Metronome*. It would appear in *Esquire* and would be the first critics' poll: the authoritative poll, because, in Goffin's words, "We know who the real experts are."

Jack Kerouac would not have been considered one of those real experts, but he was a knowledgeable jazz aficionado, a regular in the early days of bebop at Minton's Playhouse in Harlem. In *On the Road*, his narrator Sal Paradise expresses his admiration for modern jazzers George Shearing, Dexter Gordon, Wardell Gray, and Slim Gaillard. In the most extended paean to jazz in the novel, Sal and Dean Moriarty head for "the little Harlem on Folsom Street" in Oakland, California.

> Out we jumped into the warm, mad night, hearing a wild tenor-man bawling across the way, going "EE-YA! EE-YA! EE-YA!" and hands clapping to the beat and folks yelling, "Go, go, go!" Dean was already racing across the street with his thumb in the air, yelling "Blow, man, blow!" . . . It was a sawdust saloon with a small bandstand on which fellows huddled with their hats on, blowing over people's heads, a crazy place . . . the behatted tenorman was blowing at the peak of a wonderfully satisfactory free idea, a rising and falling riff that went from "EE-YA!" to a crazier "EE-de-lee-Yah!" and blasted along to the rolling crash of butt-scarred drums hammered by a brutal Negro with a bull neck who didn't give a damn about anything

but punishing his busted tubs, crash, rattle-ti-boom, crash. Uproars of music, and the tenorman *had it* and everybody knew he had it. Dean was clutching his head in the crowd, and it was a mad crowd. They were all urging that tenorman to hold it and keep with it . . . and he was raising himself from a crouch and going down again with his horn, looping it up in a clear cry above the furor. . . .

"Stay with it, man!" roared a man with a foghorn voice . . . "Whoo!" said Dean . . . Boom, kick, that drummer was kicking his drums down the cellar and rolling the beat upstairs with his murderous sticks, rattley-boom! . . . The pianist was only pounding the keys with spread-eagled fingers, chords, at intervals when the great tenorman was drawing breath for another blast—Chinese chords, shuddering the piano at every timber, chink and wire, boing! The tenorman jumped down from the platform and stood in the crowd . . . he just hauled back and stamped his feet and blew down a hoarse, laughing blast, and drew breath, and raised the horn, and blew high, wide, and screaming in the air . . . and finally . . . decided to blow his top and crouched down and held a note in high C for a long time as everything else crashed along.

The solo turns into a pas de deux between the tenorman and Dean, who is leaning into the bell of the horn and screaming exhortations, and ends in a Dionysian frenzy.

So who were Sal and Dean listening to? This would have been around 1948, when bebop was still struggling to gain acceptance on the West Coast, chiefly in Los Angeles—it would not have found its way to a "sawdust saloon" on Folsom Street (or more likely 7th Street) in Oakland. Sal and Dean would more likely have ended up in a club featuring Big Jay McNeely or someone like him. There's a famous photograph of Big Jay playing the saxophone lying on his back, while two young T-shirted white men lean over the bandstand to shout out encouragement; they could be Sal and Dean.

Dean is an overgrown juvenile delinquent engaged in a mindless pursuit of kicks, and he responds purely to the intensity of the moment; but Sal, although irresistibly drawn to follow "the only people for me . . . the mad ones, the ones who are mad to live, mad to talk, mad to be saved, desirous of everything at the same time," is also serious about jazz, and he's always a scrupulous reporter on the scenes that Dean leads him into. Here he's sucked in by Dean's ecstatic response to the music, but he's also listening closely to what's being played. He hears the "EE-YA! EE-YA!" that draws Dean in, the driving intensity that Illinois Jacquet brought into the music, but he's also aware that the tenorman is developing a "wonderfully satisfactory free idea," the "EE-YA!" evolving into "EE-de-lee-yah." He hears the crash of the drums but hears it develop into a rolling crash, punctuating a more complex "rattle-ti-boom." The piano player is playing "Chinese chords"—calling to mind Cab Calloway's definition of bebop. Sal is in his element, vicariously participating in Dean's breathless immediacy, but he is also in his own element, listening to jazz.

Why was this form of jazz, this updated swing, this jazz with a beat, not recognized as such at the time? It should have been. Big band swing had reached its zenith, and jazz audiences were ready for the next development in dance music. The big ballrooms, with a few exceptions, had become unprofitable, which meant that the big bands had lost their venues. Small groups were economically more practical, easier to keep together, and easier to travel with.

The big bands had generated and brought to the fore a number of virtuoso soloists: Lester Young with Count Basie, Illinois Jacquet with Lionel Hampton, Coleman Hawkins with Fletcher Henderson, Charlie Parker with Jay McShann, Louis Armstrong with his own groups. Other instrumentalists like Gene Krupa with Benny Goodman and Buddy Rich with Artie Shaw developed a following and started their own groups. The public's appetite for these crowd-pleasing virtuosi had been whetted. Vocalists were the most prominent. Frank Sinatra, once an afterthought in the Tommy Dorsey orchestra, was now an idol. On a somewhat smaller scale, the same was true of the instrumental soloists, and the small-group alignment was an ideal showcase for them.

So why did the small-group swing combos not command more critical respect? There are a couple of answers. First, they simply did not fit the narrative. They weren't the big swing orchestras, villains or heroes of the narrative, depending on one's point of view, or somewhere in between. They weren't the pioneers, the authentic voice of Americana, to be honored as a relic of the past. They weren't the heralds of a new age in American music, in which jazz was to take its place in the world of high art. But more than that, much of the answer lies, as is so often the case in American culture, with race. The jazz wars between the traditionalists and the swing merchants, between the progressives and the so-called moldy figs, was played out in the media, in pitched debates between the journalists, critics, and tastemakers who wrote about such matters. And those journalists, critics, and tastemakers were predominantly white.

The jazz of the 1920s and '30s had exploded into national prominence when white bands, going back as far the Original Dixieland Jass Band, and continuing through Whiteman and Goodman and Miller, began playing it. Bebop was the creation of Black artists, but it drew into its nascent sphere white musicians like Al Haig, Stan Levey, and George Wallington, soloists like Stan Getz and Lee Konitz, and bandleaders like Stan Kenton. And to the mostly white critics who wrote about these culture wars and championed one side or the other, there were two kinds of jazz: swing and bebop. The new small-group swing records that were being made by Black performers for Black audiences were mostly ignored by the critical establishment, as were the small clubs in Harlem or Central Avenue in Los Angeles or 7th Street in Oakland. White guys like Sal and Dean were very much the exception, and they were hardly influencers.

But the music was happening, developing, taking on a life of its own, and not without influence on the larger jazz world. Even Ornette Coleman started out playing in a rhythm and blues band. The progressives, who ruled the critical day, stressed innovation and complexity, sometimes at the cost of drive and immediacy. The small-group swing combos, the rhythm and blues players, the purveyors of jazz with a beat, stressed that drive and immediacy, and they captured the hearts and the hips and the dancing feet of the day.

Illinois Jacquet, who had substantial careers in both fields, looked back on that time:

> I didn't bother to read write-ups then, anyway; these things were never important to me. It was always the reaction of the people that I cared about. I've been playing among people all my life; I was a dancer once, and we've always been in show business. I always thought of the people before anybody.
>
> But most of the things they accused me of doing, like laying on my back, I've never done. It was just that I created the excitement for the saxophone, and other players went from there, and they did everything else. I was labeled for the moving and walking and hitting the high notes at the time. And being in your twenties, man, you're going to do things—that's how it is.

Small-group swing originally was categorized on the *Billboard* charts as the Harlem Hit Parade, and then as Race Records, and finally as Rhythm and Blues, which was coined by *Billboard* editor Jerry Wexler, and is the name that stuck. Rhythm and blues, once dismissed by serious critics and music historians, has in recent years come to be accepted and praised as authentic Americana, sometimes under the name of "jump blues." But the term, and the charts, included a wide swath of music. Johnny Otis took notice of this in his book, *Upside Your Head! Rhythm and Blues on Central Avenue,* where he makes the distinction between musicians of "technical ability and jazz sophistication" and those in "the traditional blues field where another form of subtle sophistication was required (witness Muddy Waters, Lightnin' Hopkins, or Memphis Minnie), but [who] were usually not equipped to function in a big modern swing band. Players who could span the gap," Otis says, "such as T-Bone Walker, Ray Charles, and Danny Barker, were rare exceptions." In recent years, that umbrella has also come to include contemporary Black music which is called R&B.

For purposes of this book, the music we'll be discussing—music that is broadly classified as rhythm and blues but made by Otis's musicians of "technical ability and jazz sophistication," the music which updated Black swing for a new era and smaller personnel—is "small-group swing."

CHAPTER ONE

Jacquet and Jordan

A new era in American music didn't suddenly emerge, fully formed, in 1942. Nothing works like that. But 1942 is a good place to start. That year, New Orleans trumpeter Bunk Johnson, rescued from obscurity and long gone from the music business (it had been a long time since anyone wanted to hear his old style), with a new trumpet and new store-bought teeth, made his first recordings, and the New Orleans revival was launched. Charlie Parker's solos on "Hootie Blues" and "Sepian Bounce" made it onto the jukeboxes, and musicians everywhere could hear what those who had been privileged to hear the McShann orchestra experienced and what everyone who had heard it was talking about. And in 1942, Illinois Jacquet recorded "Flying Home" with the Lionel Hampton orchestra, and Louis Jordan had his first top ten, then his first number one hit on the Harlem Hit Parade: records that did not enter into the discussion of what constituted real jazz, but which created a baseline for a new music that would keep jazz thriving, though unheralded as such, as a popular art form in the 1940s.

Lionel Hampton was known as one of the great showmen in jazz, and when he left Benny Goodman to front his own orchestra, he had the showcase to demonstrate it. Drummer Roy Brooks recalls: "[Hampton] was a drummer also and he would drum on a tom tom a littler bigger than this, and he'd get up on that drum and dance. Now I've never seen too many people dance on a drum. He may be the only drummer I've seen dance on a drum. But he'd do a jig on a drum, sometimes he'd fall through and jump up out." When Illinois Jacquet joined Hampton, "Flying Home" was already one of the band's most popular numbers. The melody was inspired by Hampton's first plane ride with the Goodman orchestra. He was whistling to keep his nervousness at bay, and Goodman heard him and recognized a good thing. "Flying Home" became a hit for the Goodman sextet, with a bravura solo by Charlie Christian, the formidable young guitarist who introduced some new, modern elements to the Goodman sound, then died young. So the tune was already a crowd pleaser when Hampton took it with him and made it his signature song. With the Hampton orchestra, it became a virtual show stopper, with audience response goading the band to chorus after chorus.

So when young Jacquet was given the solo assignment for the May 1942 recording session, he had big shoes to fill. There had been Goodman's recording, then a version by the Charlie Barnet orchestra. Hampton's band had already put it to wax once, with an ensemble that featured Ziggy Elman on trumpet, and between that and the live performances, it had become the jewel in the crown of the Hampton repertoire.

The lineup on May 26 was an impressive one; Hampton always had a keen eye for talent. Besides Jacquet on tenor sax, there was Dexter Gordon. Jack McVea, later to be one of the stars of the race records charts, was on baritone. Hampton's right-hand man, Marshal Royal, was the first alto saxophone, and his younger brother Ernie was on trumpet, along with Joe Newman. Influential pianist Milt Buckner was Hampton's staff arranger.

Whatever "Flying Home" had been in the past, from the moment this version was released, it was *the* version. It was the solo people wanted to hear. Later tenormen for Hampton, including Gordon and Arnett Cobb, played that solo. (Hampton would record it in 1944 with Cobb as "Flying Home #2.") It has been credited with being the seminal touchstone of rhythm and blues, and even as the birth of rock and roll. It inspired the wild improvisation that Sal Paradise and Dean Moriarty heard in that jazz club in Oakland.

Jean-Baptiste Jacquet was born in Broussard, Louisiana, but at an early age he moved with his family to Houston, where the French name became too difficult for the locals to pronounce, so he came to be called by his middle name, "Illinois," chosen for him for reasons that are only vaguely remembered. In some accounts, he was given the name by his mother, a Sioux Indian, as a corruption of the Sioux word for "superior man," and by others, he was named to honor a friend of his mother who came down from Chicago to help out with the new baby. His father, a railroad worker, was musical, playing part-time in a big band, and his three older brothers all played instruments. Illinois began as a three-year-old tap

Figure 1.1. Illinois Jacquet, New York, ca. May 1947. William P. Gottlieb Collection, Library of Congress, Music Division.

dancer performing in front of his father's band, then took up the drums, switching to trumpet when he figured out that playing the drums meant having a whole lot of stuff to pack up and carry around. But hearing Lester Young and Herschel Evans with the Count Basie band sealed it for him: "I knew that I was going to be a saxophone player."

Jacquet began on the alto sax, and by fifteen he had secured a job with Milt Larkin, who had one of the better territorial bands operating out of Houston. Larkin's band included future jazz luminaries Arnett Cobb, Eddie "Cleanhead" Vinson, and Wild Bill Davis, all of whom would make names for themselves in the coming decades playing jazz with a beat. Jacquet developed a reputation for his precociousness as much as his playing ability. As he told Jeff McCord, an interviewer from *Texas Monthly*, "Every band that came through heard about this young guy and would want to jam with me." From those experiences, he learned that he could hold his own with anyone. That knowledge, along with increasing anger at the strict segregation of Texas in the 1930s, led him to pull up stakes at seventeen and head for Los Angeles, where he found new and exciting musical stimulation, but not much in the way of an escape from racism. McCord described what happened at one of his first gigs: "He joined up with a mercurial bassist named Charles Mingus, and while setting up in a bar for their first gig, a patron called out, 'What are you n*****s doing here?' Mingus cracked the guy over the head with his bass. 'There went that job,' Jacquet recalled." Jacquet renewed a friendship with T-Bone Walker and became friends with a highly regarded but as yet little known jazz pianist named Nat "King" Cole. When Lionel Hampton tried to recruit Cole for his orchestra, Cole passed on the offer but recommended Jacquet. Hampton liked what he heard, but he already had two alto players, so he convinced Jacquet to switch to the tenor—a fortuitous choice.

"Flying Home" was the only solo Jacquet ever recorded with the Hampton band, but it was enough to brand him. Every club date, every theater date—every set on every date—the audience wanted "Flying Home." And they wanted the kid with the tenor sax to step up and knock 'em dead. It got to be too overwhelming for the youngster, who was also very much aware that he was on salary and not sharing in the windfall that was sweeping into the Hampton coffers in response to his epochal solo. In 1943, he said "I looked in the mirror and said, 'You're dying and [Hampton is] getting rich,'" and so he quit the band.

Jacquet's next job was with Cab Calloway, and life was simpler, if not necessarily everything he would have wanted musically. Calloway was famous for paying his musicians a living wage and paying them on time. He was also famous for being a strict disciplinarian and for making his musicians play strictly by the book. There were no ecstatic honking solos in Cab's orchestra; in fact, there were no solos. There was only one star, and that was the guy out in front, in the tails and the conked-down hair, singing "Hi-de-hi-de-hi-de hi-de-ho." "Flying Home" was strictly not a part of the Calloway repertoire.

But if Jacquet had opted out of the limelight, the music scene on Central Avenue in Los Angeles had progressed without him and in his image. The excitement of his honking, driving tenor sax solos had spread. At the same time, on the East Coast, the fame of another young saxophone player was spreading, and his lightning-fast, chord-inverting, rhythm-defying improvisational solos were the talk of Minton's Playhouse and Monroe's Uptown House in Harlem and the downtown houses along 52nd Street.

In 1944, Charlie Parker had not yet come to LA, and his 1945 club date with Dizzy Gillespie at Billy Berg's, to a decidedly mixed reaction, was still a blip on the horizon. But it was anything but a blip on the East Coast, where the jazz critics and the tastemakers hung their fedoras. The new New York music (not yet bebop) was the hot news, not some honking tenor sax players out in Hollywood somewhere. (Joke of the era: "What's the difference between Los Angeles and yogurt? Yogurt has a living culture.")

But on Central Avenue there was a living culture, and in Watts and even up in Oakland, where it was waiting to be discovered by Jack Kerouac, who was not yet one of those tastemakers, even if that culture existed under the radar of *DownBeat* and *Metronome*. It was a time of restless exploration for jazz musicians, from bebop to the new trends in swing, which used Jacquet's solo as one of its chief inspirations. Jacquet could not stay out of it for long. Leaving Calloway, he started finding his way back into the scene, assembling his own small group, as well as playing with his old friend Charles Mingus, who had been working regularly in a group led by Jacquet's brother Russell. Jacquet also crossed paths with other musicians, including Lester Young, and began to jam with Lester at an impromptu but regular Sunday afternoon session organized by a promoter named Norman Granz.

Lester's brother Lee Young, a drummer, was one of the regulars at Granz's Sunday sessions. He put together one of the early small-group swing groups. In *Central Avenue Sounds*, a collection of oral histories, he gives an excellent account of how that sound was created:

> My band sounded like a huge band; it was a seven-piece band, but it sounded like twelve because of the way the band was written for. When Lester came in the band, that's what gave us our bigger sound, because we used two tenors and put the guitar on top. That's electric guitar; that gives you a lot of sound. And the trumpet. So we had four parts, but we had a heavy bottom because of the two tenors. And they would spread the voicing so it really sounded big. That band was very, very unique. We rehearsed six days a week, and we learned one arrangement per day. And we never did read music on the bandstand. And the band always stood up. That was the uniqueness of the band. The only people that sat down were the drummer and the pianist. The guitarist stood up, because

Figure 1.2. Lester Young, Famous Door, New York, ca. September 1946. William P. Gottlieb Collection, Library of Congress, Music Division.

he was on the front line with the horns. And musicians would come from all of the studios to hear us. They said, "These guys don't ever read any music." We had great people doing these arrangements for us.

Lee Young captures a number of the things that made this music different. The size of the group is important, but that's not all. In the traditional big band, a section—the saxophones, the trombones—would stand up briefly to play a part, then sit down again. Young, and the other musicians pioneering this new style, made a conscious decision to go against that tradition—as Young says, "that was the uniqueness of the band." But it was really the uniqueness of this style. They were on their feet, ready for action, along with the dancers. They didn't read music. Not because they couldn't—most of the musicians, and certainly all of the Los Angeles natives like the Young brothers, had a lot of schooling behind them. But rehearsing as they did, knowing their parts, knowing when the improvisation was going to come, meant that they had one less barrier between them and their audiences. It meant they could move: as Illinois Jacquet did, much to the disapproval of some critics; as the Oakland tenor player who blew for Sal Paradise and Dean Moriarty did; as Big Jay McNeely would do to an extreme—becoming part of the ecstatic communion of the dancers and listeners.

The culture of Watts and Central Avenue was not to everyone's taste. Racism was still rampant in Los Angeles in this period. One way that it expressed itself was through the anger directed at the Black and Latino male fashion of the zoot suit and the charge that it was unpatriotic to wear the flashy, loose-fitting outfit that took up yards of cloth that could have gone into the war effort. This culminated in the "zoot suit riots" of June 1943, when thousands of whites, many of them servicemen from nearby bases, roamed the streets of Los Angeles, beating up zoot suit–wearing Blacks and Latinos and tearing off their clothes. The race-fueled attacks did not stop with zoot suit wearers, and the overwhelmingly white Los Angeles police mostly responded by arresting racial minorities.

In July of 1944, Granz organized a benefit concert at the Philharmonic Auditorium for Mexican youths who had been arrested during the zoot suit riots. He got Nat "King" Cole and Les Paul to headline. Other featured performers were Jacquet, Jack McVea, J. J. Johnson, Meade Lux Lewis, Joe Sullivan, Buddy Rich, Red Callender, and Lee Young. The event was named "A Jazz Concert at the Philharmonic Auditorium," but space demands on the flyers and print ads forced Granz to shorten that to "Jazz at the Philharmonic." At the concert, Jacquet went out onstage a featured player but came back a star.

He had learned a few things since Lionel Hampton had handed him a tenor saxophone that was so big he was not even sure he could hold it. After practicing and beginning to master the conventional fingering of the instrument, he put some of his earlier training to work and found that if he used clarinet fingering, he could reach a high A natural with little effort, and from there, he could move into an upper register not previously associated with the robust instrument.

Building on his "Flying Home" success, breaking free from the straitjacket of the Calloway horn section, he let loose, honking, growling, taking his saxophone into its upper registers and beyond, feeding off the excitement of the crowd. And excitement there was. "That particular style really came out," he said in a 1973 interview with Les Tomkins for the National Jazz Archive. "The things that had been cooped up in me sort of caused an explosion, and the crowd would be all for excitement. So we just create anything like that as we go; no one plans it." He got the applause, and he fed off it.

This was a jazz crowd. They'd come to hear the sophisticated progressive piano of Nat Cole, the boogie-woogie mastery of Meade Lux Lewis, the pioneering trombone bebop of J. J. Johnson, the guitar wizardry of Les Paul. But they loved the ecstatic intensity, the bravura wailing and note-holding of a new jazz star, Illinois Jacquet. Granz released Jacquet's "Blues, Part 2," originally on Disc Records, with the performance credited to Norman Granz's Jazz at the Philharmonic although Jacquet was the star performer. The lineup features Jacquet and Jack McVea on tenor sax; J. J. Johnson, trombone; "Shorty" Nadine, piano; Johnny Miller, bass; Les Paul, guitar; and Lee Young, drums. Jacquet can be heard urging his saxophone to such extended high notes that at one point he actually seems to reach above the threshold of human hearing.

In 1945, with the Petrillo strike ended and companies signing up recording artists again, Jacquet made his first recording under his own name for the Los Angeles label Philo Records, which quickly changed its name to Aladdin; it would become known for releasing new sounds in jazz from established stars like Lester Young and the new jazz with a beat, from artists like Jacquet and Wynonie Harris (whose initial outing for Aladdin featured Teddy Edwards and Howard McGhee in a band led by Johnny Otis), all of it marketed to Black audiences. Jacquet's first 78 RPM single for Aladdin was a two-sided version of "Flying Home," with a band that included his brother Russell on trumpet, Henry Coker on trombone, Sir Charles Thompson on piano, and Johnny Otis on drums.[1]

For Apollo Records, another one of the new independent labels specializing in Black music, he recorded Eubie Blake's "Memories of You," a popular ballad that had been widely recorded by both sweet and hot orchestras, including Lionel Hampton's. Jacquet's group included brother Russell, Charles Mingus, and Bill Doggett. The flip side is "Merle's Mood," a Jacquet original, a swing number in which Jacquet gets a little wild but not over the top. "Bottoms Up," recorded in January 1946 for Apollo with the same musicians, was the flip side of an instrumental version of "Ghost of a Chance," the popular Bing Crosby ballad with music by Victor Young. "Ghost of a Chance" has some lovely playing on it, but it was "Bottoms Up" that really made people sit up and take notice. It was the real thing,

Figure 1.3. Norman Granz, ca. May 1947. William P. Gottlieb Collection, Library of Congress, Music Division.

the new driving sound in small-group swing, and the prototype for what followed for so many bandleaders and tenor saxophone players.

Norman Granz continued to present his all-star jam sessions, with such artists as Charlie Parker, Lester Young, and Oscar Peterson—a cornucopia of jazz immortals. And Jacquet continued to be one of the regulars and continued to delight audiences. However, he was not such a hit with the critics. This was the era when jazz criticism was getting serious, which meant taking itself seriously. Peter Townsend, in his book *Pearl Harbor Jazz: Change in Popular Music in the Early 1940s*, notes this trend:

> As the prestige of the newly defined form rose . . . Jazz was now regarded as inherently separate from its earlier mixed associations, so that a performer like Fats Waller was seen as

consisting of two incompatible functions, "serious jazz artist" and "entertainer." In the same way, postabstraction jazz discourse saw the long-time association of bands like Duke Ellington's with entertainers, dancers and on-stage movies as a historic slight upon his dignity . . .

The consensus around jazz . . . was formed at a time when there were persuasive critical forces denigrating popular music and culture. Jazz criticism did not in the 1940s, and has not since, come to an accommodation with popular culture, as has the study of film, which is comfortable with the idea that there can be great creativity and power of expression within popular forms. For writers on jazz, there has been no way of taking a popular form like jazz seriously without taking it *seriously*.

The line between serious jazz and music that couldn't be called jazz because it wasn't serious enough has always been a delicate one for critics to navigate. Cab Calloway's flamboyance and showmanship tend to rule him out as a jazzman, and jazz historians often treat the time that musicians like Dizzy Gillespie spent in his band as a youthful indiscretion, not part of Gillespie's growth and development. But Jacquet, reminiscing about his early days with Tomkins, cites not "mere entertainer" Calloway but "real jazz musician" Hampton, as the inspiration for his own crowd-pleasing stage presence: "As well as being a great musician, he's one of the greatest showmen you'll ever run across in the music business. It rubbed off on me, although it was already there; he just ensured that it was expressed, that's all."

Jacquet's career lasted a long time. In 1946 he moved to New York and joined the Count Basie orchestra, replacing Lester Young. He also organized, toured, and recorded with his own small groups. In the 1980s, sensing the public's readiness for it, he organized a big swing band and led it for the next two decades. He lived to become the first jazz musician to be named an artist in residence at Harvard University and to play a duet with Bill Clinton at a 1993 inaugural gala. He gave his last performance in 2004, shortly before his death. By that time, he was revered as a jazz master, but that did not mean that critics were ready to recognize his early work being in the jazz tradition. Instead, the consensus was that he had "matured."

Which, of course, he had. You don't do anything the same way when you're fifty as you did when you were twenty. As he told Tomkins,

"Now the young kids are playing like that, and I don't even play like that no more. Isn't that funny? It just shows you—when you're young, you're young." But his influence reached down over the years. Young saxophonist James Carter, interviewed at the 2015 Newport Jazz Festival, talked about his regret that he never got to play with Illinois Jacquet:

> I missed the chance to tell him how vital he was, taking the tenor saxophone to the next level of virility beyond Coleman Hawkins. He was really the prototype for what they called the honkers and . . . you know . . . he set the pace for Willis Jackson, Big Jay McNeely, [Frank] "Floorshow" Culley, all the cats—Clarence Clemons—he laid the blueprint out for us. He widened the sensibility [of the tenor saxophone]—it had some sass, it had some joy, exuberance—all of these things could be brought to the tenor, and it's immediately identifiable to the listener.[2]

Illinois Jacquet was a child of the 1940s, the small-group swing era. He got his start with Lionel Hampton, but Hampton, one of the most savvy musicians of his time, knew that there was a new direction in music coming, and it was no accident that he hired the nineteen-year-old alto player, switched him to tenor, and gave him the lead solo on his remake of his most popular tune. Hampton was still working with a big band in 1941, but he was laying the groundwork for the sound that would be developed in the smaller aggregations of the 1940s.

Louis Jordan, on the other hand, was a veteran of the big band era. He began his career with the Rabbit Foot Minstrels, a band that toured the Southern tent circuit. He recorded with ensembles put together by Clarence Williams. Playing with Charlie Gaines, a bandleader who had split off from Williams, he toured with, and even recorded with, Louis Armstrong.

His vocal on a Gaines recording, "I Can't Dance, I Got Ants in My Pants," gave Jordan his big break. Chick Webb's orchestra covered the tune and also hired Jordan away as an alto saxophonist and vocalist. So when Jordan started his own group after Webb's death, he was bringing the experience of big band swing with him and very consciously setting out to recreate the Webb sound with a small ensemble.

Jordan was hired by Webb right around the same time that the bandleader signed Ella Fitzgerald, which meant that he was not likely to

Figure 1.4. Louis Jordan and his group, ca. 1946–48. William P. Gottlieb Collection, Library of Congress, Music Division.

get the lion's share of vocal assignments. Fitzgerald quickly established herself as considerably more than just another big band vocalist, while Jordan, at this point, *was* just another big band vocalist, using the sweet tenor that was popular in those days. Jordan was also featured in some trio recordings with Fitzgerald, but listening to them, one can't help but wish that the other two would just shut up and let Miss Ella sing.

John Hammond, impresario/producer and, in those days, music critic for *DownBeat*, had attacked Webb for "elaborate, badly written 'white' arrangements."[3] It's hard to understand what Hammond was talking about, but he could have had Jordan in mind. As a vocalist in 1937, he had more in common with someone like Bob Eberly of the Jimmy Dorsey band than with the hip, racially aware figure he was to become. Hammond also had a dismissive word for the band's " 'comedian' saxophonist." In 1937, he was already looking forward to Leonard Feather's definitions of jazz as a serious art form, not to be made sport of by saxophone-playing comedians.

Nonetheless, in 1937, Webb's band was the hottest thing in New York. The Savoy Ballroom, on Lenox Avenue between 140th and 141st Streets in Harlem, had opened its doors in 1926 and had quickly become the premier venue in town, the in spot for dancing. Fletcher Henderson and his orchestra opened; Benny Goodman, Count Basie, and Duke Ellington all played there. But the orchestra favored by the dancers and listeners who crowded the Savoy Ballroom was the one led by the little hunchbacked drummer. Samuel B. Charters and Leonard Kunstadt, in their book *Jazz: A History of the New York Scene*, describe Webb's influence:

> Chick was the first drummer to attract a large jazz audience and his style influenced most of the drummers who followed him. He was an exciting soloist, but even more exciting as an ensemble drummer. He drove the band with his strong, steady, bass-drum beat, accenting the rhythm with every part of his set . . . he had extraordinary control of dynamics, shading his beat to the softest instrumental level . . . At its highest level, when the band was riding out a Savoy "flag raiser," his play was a slashing display of ferocious drive and he lifted the entire band to ferocious heights. The audiences loved him, and he returned their enthusiasm with a deep warmth and affection.

The Chick Webb gig was the peak of Jordan's career to date, a huge step up from everything he had done before. It was a learning experience for him and also a showcase. As a vocalist with the band, and enough of a personality to be attacked by Hammond, he was feeling enough of the limelight to know he wanted more of it. Jordan was always a diligent student and a hard worker. He absorbed everything about the Webb band, showmanship and musicianship both. He was already thinking about starting an ensemble of his own. Jordan told interviewers in later years that he stayed with Webb until the little drummer's death in 1939. More likely, he was fired by Webb in 1938. As he started making plans to start his own band, the first place he recruited from was Webb's orchestra.

Nineteen-year-old Ella Fitzgerald was Webb's protégé and almost like a daughter to him—it was rumored that Webb and his wife had adopted the teenager, a rumor that Webb did not try too hard to deny. It was good publicity. However, Fitzgerald and Jordan had a different bond: they conducted a torrid affair, in spite of the fact that Jordan was already married (apparently to two different women). Jordan was not above putting these conflicting loyalties to the test, approaching Fitzgerald about leaving Webb to join his new band. If that had happened, jazz history would have been significantly rewritten. But it did not, and Webb was not amused.

It seems more likely that Jordan left Webb's band in 1938, although he could have freelanced on his own while still with Webb. In any event, he appears to have recorded with a group of his own, backing up blues singer Rodney Sturgis, on two 1938 records for Decca, which would become his longtime label. The first, "Toodle Loo on Down/The Gal That Wrecked My Life," credited to Sturgis with Lovie [sic] Jordon's Elks Rendezvous Band, was recorded in late 1938. In January 1939 he was back in the studio with Sturgis recording "So Good/Away from You," and they got a little closer to his name—this time it was Louie Jordon's Elks Rendezvous Band. Jordan was still very much a work in progress. "So Good" has a minimal and conventional blues backing. "Toodle Loo" has a couple of nice sax breaks in the swing tradition, and "The Gal That Wrecked My Life" features an accompaniment reminiscent of the kind Louis Armstrong gave to blues singers a decade earlier.

Sturgis seems to have disappeared after these two records, so presumably they weren't successful, although he was quite good,[4] but Jordan apparently made enough of an impression that Decca continued recording him, under his correct spelling and his preferred band name, the Tympany Five. None of this was arbitrary or accidental, not even the apparent misspelling in the band's name. Jordan knew what a tympani was—he used one on his early records—but he liked the *y* on the end, with its suggestion of "symphony." He was set with the name that would become his brand, although he dropped the tympani from the ensemble fairly early on, and he seldom if ever had a quintet—more often six, seven, or eight musicians.

Unlike Jacquet, who went with the moment, responded to audiences, and played on instinct, Jordan planned everything. His bands were rehearsed so exhaustively that musicians who couldn't handle the grueling rehearsal schedule sometimes quit the band. Jacquet was nineteen when he made his breakthrough with "Flying Home." Jordan was thirty when he made his first recording with his own band and thirty-four when he had his first number one hit.

And the handful of years' difference in their first recordings also made a big difference. "Flying Home" was cut in June 1942. Pearl Harbor had happened. War was ravaging Europe and the Pacific, the home front had gone into overdrive manufacturing war materiel. There was a new urgency in the air. 1938 was still very much the swing era, and Jordan was not so much trying to break new ground as to be part of what was happening. The sound was swing, and Jordan showed his versatility, playing baritone and tenor sax and clarinet as well as his alto, experimenting with different voicings . . . and different voices. On the Fats Waller / Andy Razaf classic "Honeysuckle Rose," his phrasing is reminiscent of Louis Armstrong. Jordan continued to record for Decca over the next few years, having enough success that the label kept him on, developing and refining his style. He went on a different route from any other jazz musician you can think of—different from the moderns, different from the standard bearers for swing.

Most of the other swing musicians—including forward-looking bandleaders like Hampton, Cootie Williams, and Chick Webb up to his death—were still wedded to the idea that you needed a big band—that audiences would demand the sound and the presence of a big band, the assurance that they were getting their money's worth. The moderns played in small combos, but they also played in small venues. They were in a whole different sphere, both musically and economically.

Jordan had set himself the task of creating a small combo sound that would compete with the big bands. This was not so difficult on record. Recording techniques were much less sophisticated. Records were released on 78 RPM shellac discs; they were played on gramophones that used phonograph needles that had to be replaced frequently but generally weren't (sometimes teenagers would use straight pins if they were out of needles), so they were scratchy and rife with surface noise. Or they were played on a newly popular device, the jukebox, where a hit record would wear out its grooves, or on a newly popular radio format, the disc jockey show, where they could be heard over tinny, staticky AM radios. So the fullness of a big band was less important than a catchy tune, a persuasive singer, and a hot soloist.

The early Decca recordings from 1938 to 1941 are enjoyable listening and an interesting study. Jordan developed, early on, that feel of big band swing with a small group. The tympani gave his ensemble a recognizable signature sound, but one that was ultimately limiting, and it's not hard to understand why he dropped it. At this stage, his vocals were similar to those of a big band vocalist. They play as a part of the ensemble, not distinct from it, and are not the focal point—his saxophone solo on "Doug the Jitterbug," for example, is more distinctive than his vocal solo. And indeed, on several of his early recordings, he hands the vocal duties off to someone else.

But if he could compete with the big bands on wax, live performance, still a band's economic backbone, was another story. To play the big venues like the Savoy or Roseland in New York, the Trianon in Chicago, the Trocadero in Hollywood, or the myriad other venues in small cities and towns all across America, you had to compete with Goodman, the Dorseys, Ellington, Cab Calloway, Horace Heidt, Guy Lombardo, or Lawrence Welk. That was Jordan's challenge. He met it with the perfectionism that was his hallmark. Not just the endless rehearsals of the music but rehearsals of stage movements—the whole band was choreographed. He had the sharpest band uniforms, the shiniest shoes. And just as importantly, he worked on the stage business he had begun to develop as the " 'comedian' saxophonist" in Webb's orchestra. John Hammond may not have liked it, but the audiences at the Savoy certainly did, and Jordan's priority was playing for the people. So as much as he studied Webb's arrangements and tempi, he was also studying Calloway's stage presence.

Here's another way that Jordan differed from the other musicians who were developing the new jazz sound for the 1940s. They were honing their craft, stretching their art, measuring their virtuosity against their peers and compatriots at Minton's Playhouse or Monroe's Uptown House in Harlem. Jordan was doing his own version of the same thing at the Fox Head Tavern in Cedar Rapids, Iowa. As biographer Stephen Koch puts it:

> With its middle-America location and lack of extracurricular activities (especially for black musicians), it was perfect for [Jordan] to hone the music that would appeal across demographics. The band was free to improvise, experiment with new material and clown, away from the scrutiny of their musician peers. Further, it was home to heretofore-untapped audience segments—the band hadn't played much for largely rural, white audiences. During the Tympany Five's residency there, the Fox Head's owner let them rehearse at the club during the day. For once, band members welcomed rehearsals. Stage routines built around songs became almost as important as the songs themselves. "The Fox Head in Cedar Rapids was a great turning point in my career," [Jordan] would later recall.

Jordan made a couple of important career moves as the '40s began, aligning himself with booking agent Berle Adams and producer Milt Gabler. Adams would go on to represent many of the top names in jazz (including Illinois Jacquet), but Jordan was his first big success story, and their association would last the decade. Adams booked him into some of the top venues in Chicago, as an opening act for the Mills Brothers and then as a headliner. He encouraged him to work on his showmanship, particularly his comedic skills. Milt Gabler had parlayed his work with his own independent label to a job producing for Decca. He worked on Lionel Hampton/Illinois Jacquet's "Flying Home" and numerous other sessions with Decca's major artists. Some of his most creative involvement, though, was with Jordan, fine-tuning his style to bring him back into the studio, ready to reach for a new level of success, which would be forthcoming rapidly. Jordan's first recording with Gabler was "What's the Use of Getting Sober (When You're Gonna Get Drunk Again")."

Most of the fine-tuning had already been done by Jordan, in front of sophisticated Chicago audiences and small-town Iowa audiences, in front of Blacks and whites and (rarely) mixed crowds. But here it all came together: Jordan's vocals becoming the main focus, broad and attention-grabbing comedy, the rhythm of swing updated to a shuffle beat. "What's the Use of Getting Sober" went to number one on the Harlem Hit Parade, the first of many for Jordan and the Tympany Five.

Jordan had developed a new sound, one that would be influential beyond his imagining. Its influence would lead to his being called the father of rock and roll, which is not a sobriquet that's conducive to being taken seriously as a jazz musician. Actually, by the late 1950s, when rock and roll had taken over the world, much to the consternation of a generation that had shocked their elders by dancing to swing, Jordan had taken a step back in time. He had formed a big band and was playing classic swing (he was out of step with the times, and the venture was not successful). But his claim to rock and roll patrimony comes largely from his updating of swing patterns into a shuffle beat.

Jordan certainly didn't invent the shuffle. Its origins, like the origins of most musical forms, are lost to history, going back (some say) to early dances performed by enslaved people. But Jordan's use of it influenced much of the new small-group swing sounds of the 1940s, the music that came to be pigeonholed as rhythm and blues. Milt Gabler took Jordan's shuffle beat virtually whole, but emphasized the back beat more strongly, and gave it to a white country and western group he had just signed to Decca in 1954. Gabler's schooling of Bill Haley and the Comets paid off, and "Rock Around the Clock" became the new national sensation.

There's a point at which music really does morph into something completely different. There is a complete disconnect between the backbeat of Bill Haley and the Comets and the swing rhythms of Chick Webb, even if Louis Jordan is their six degrees of separation. Other degrees of separation are harder to pin down. The jazz traditionalists argued that it had happened with swing: the music lost the syncopation, the rhythmic looseness, the openness to improvisation of real jazz. And this was probably true of some of the dance bands of the 1930s but certainly not true of Goodman and Webb, Henderson, and Jimmie Lunceford.

Did the shuffle rhythms of Louis Jordan pervert the rhythms of jazz? There's not such a hard and fast line. Drummer Eric Parker[5] explains the blurred line of difference between the swing and shuffle rhythms:

> Swing is a bit looser, with more breath between the notes, and a shuffle is a bit more boxed up. There are many variations and shadings between the two. For example, I can either play a shuffle rhythm on cymbal and snare, or play a jazz swing rhythm on the cymbal while the snare remains in a tight shuffle. That's my favorite version, because I can "dial in" the amount of swing-to-shuffle ratio with cymbal pattern and snare/ bass drum pattern depending on the song/tempo/musical environment/musicians I'm playing with and the volume we should be playing according to the size room we're in.

A couple of other factors went into the dismissal of small-group swing, particularly as practiced by Jordan, from the definitions of jazz that were being formulated in the early 1940s and haven't changed much since. One is Jordan's vocals. Jazz theoreticians have never known quite what to do with vocals—hence the endless arguments over "is Frank Sinatra a jazz singer?" Those vocalists who are undeniably jazz singers, like Sarah Vaughan, are often described as having a voice like a horn. Singers like Dinah Washington—who could sing the blues, sing with beboppers, or sing pop or rock and roll with equal facility—tend to confuse the theoreticians, and their best solution is to pretend the other recordings don't exist and concentrate on the ones where she "sounds like a horn."

As noted here, on Jordan's early recordings with the Elks Rendez-vous Band and the Tympany Five, he sounds like part of the ensemble, a typical swing band vocalist. On his mature recordings of the 1940s, he has stepped out in front, like Frank Sinatra or Bing Crosby. Should that disqualify him as a jazz musician? Only by the narrowest of definitions, and you really can't make a definition narrow enough. Tony Bennett, in his recordings with Bill Evans and Count Basie, is a real jazz singer, and he's still Tony Bennett. Ella Fitzgerald, Sarah Vaughan, Nancy Wilson, Billie Holiday all straddled the line between jazz and pop . . . or why not go back in time? Louis Armstrong was the living definition of everything that mattered about jazz, and his singing was the focal point as far back as "Sweethearts on Parade" in 1932 or "I Can't Give You Anything but Love" in 1929.

Then there's Jordan's comedy, the novelty songs: "Five Guys Named Moe," "Saturday Night Fish Fry," and "Beware Brother Beware." Comedy is always hard for the serious art folks to deal with, which is why Fats Waller has always been such a problem. His musicianship was impossible to deny, but that clowning? And this is not just true in jazz, which is why country singer George Jones is showered with plaudits and awards for his heartfelt treatment of love lost, "He Stopped Loving Her Today," but not so much for another treatment of the same theme, "Yabba Dabba Doo (The King Is Gone and So Are You)." Anyway, if the Nobel Prize committee can honor writers who traffic in humor, like Dario Fo and Bob Dylan, surely there's room for it in jazz.

Some of the musicians who played with Jordan in the 1940s and early '50s had serious jazz credentials, including: Dallas Bartley, bass (who played with Earl Hines, Cab Calloway, Duke Ellington, Dinah Washington, Ray Charles, and others); Wilmore "Slick" Jones, drums, and Al Morgan, bass (Fats Waller, Coleman Hawkins, Cab Calloway); Wild Bill Davis, keyboards (Duke Ellington, Johnny Hodges, Earl Hines, Lionel Hampton; Davis is credited with creating the organ sound from which soul jazz sprung); and guitarists Carl Hogan, Mickey Baker, and Bill Jennings.

Jordan's July 1942 session with Milt Gabler produced a string of hits, including "Five Guys Named Moe," which kept Jordan on the charts through the musicians' strike years of 1943–44, augmented by recordings made on V-discs, which were recordings made solely for distribution to the armed forces. There were also movie appearances,[6] which gave him more exposure. Decca was the first label to settle with the union, in September

1943, giving Jordan and other Decca artists a leg up in getting new music before the public. Topical songs like "Ration Blues" and "G. I. Jive" gave him a huge following among military personnel.

By the end of 1944 the recording industry was back in full swing, and Jordan was still at the top of the heap. But the musical scene, especially the Black musical scene, had changed dramatically, and Jacquet and Jordan were greatly responsible for that change.

CHAPTER TWO

The War Years

Los Angeles's Central Avenue

One important reason why the jazz establishment overlooked the new small-group swing bands was geographical. *DownBeat* and *Metronome* were mostly focused on New York; *Billboard* was more national in scope, but jazz was a very small part of its focus. The major labels (with the exception of Capitol, founded in 1942) were all headquartered in New York. The movie industry made Hollywood the center of national interest, with night clubs featuring the biggest names in the music business. But Hollywood was a tight white enclave, and show business publications that covered it had no interest in the Black part of town.

The new dance music that was evolving from swing was not limited to the West Coast, but California, and particularly Los Angeles, was a crucial center for its development. Jacquet had first come to prominence there, first with Lionel Hampton and then on his own. Hampton, as well, was a strong influence. Jordan was a national star, but in those early years his influence was felt most strongly on the West Coast. A fourth important figure, also Los Angeles–based, was Nat "King" Cole, who got his start on Central Avenue with the King Kolax Orchestra. Kolax did not stay in Los Angeles, but Cole did, working with a trio in clubs up and down Central Avenue until he made it big—and even then, returning to work the avenue's vibrant music scene. Alto sax player Marshal Royal recalls a battle of the bands on three flatbed trucks along Central as part of the annual Labor Day parade: Count Basie, Jimmie Lunceford, and a big band of local stars with the King Cole trio as the rhythm section. Cole's influences were Earl Hines, Art Tatum, and Teddy Wilson, and he also picked up on some of the modern sounds. Later, he became a beloved crooner of pop ballads. But while his career did not follow the path of the new Black swing, he was a strong influence on musicians who did.

As Lester Young's brother Lee, a jazz drummer and a mainstay of the Los Angeles jazz scene, remembered Central Avenue: "It was like a West Coast Fifty-second Street, but you never really heard of Los Angeles that much, then, where music was concerned. Everybody thought all the jazz and all the better jazz musicians came from the east. The writers from *Metronome* and *DownBeat* used to segregate it."

No mainstream music journalists were seeking out Central Avenue. Johnny Otis, in his nostalgic memoir *Upside Your Head! Rhythm and Blues on Central Avenue*, discusses this with musician/music entrepreneur Dootsie Williams:

> **D.W.** We had good writers, but we couldn't get published . . . I mean, by any major publishers. A lot of people doing a lot of good things but no way to preserve the history of it.

> **J.O.** We had good writers, and a lot of them, too—people like Abie Robinson, Almena Lomax, Lil Cumber, Joe "Smoke Rings" Harris, Stanley Robinson, Pat Alexander, Wendell Green, Gertrude Gibson, Colonel Leon Washington, Mrs. Charlotta Bass, Brad Pie Jr., Herman Hill, but they seldom, if ever, saw the light of day in the mainstream press . . . that is to say, in the white press, in actual book form.

It has been written, often, how the segregation of the first part of the twentieth century had the perhaps unintended effect of enriching a community. The doctors, lawyers, and urban professionals who couldn't move to the white suburbs stayed in the inner cities, where they became neighbors and role models to the children of poorer families. So, too, the musicians who lived and worked in South Central worked together, socialized together, rejoiced in each other's successes. And they were influenced by all the music they heard.

Johnny Otis describes his exposure, as a teenager, to just such an experience. His awakening came in Oakland, in a community similar to LA's South Central, where young John Veliotes, the son of Greek immigrants, grew up in a largely Black neighborhood and absorbed the music and culture that was to shape his life. He had been playing in a band led by an older teen who was called Count Otis Matthews—"Count," because, like Basie, he played the piano. Matthews was a Mississippi immigrant, a "down home boogie woogie barrelhouse" piano player who formed a band called the West Oakland House Rockers that played music for dancing on Saturday night. When Matthews decided to form a band, he enlisted his buddy Otis, telling him, "You're going to be the drummer, so let's find you a set of drums." He also told Otis, "You only need to learn to play one thing—'Shave and a Haircut—Six Bits.'" That lesson served Otis well in 1958 when he set out to make a rock and roll hit record, "Willie and the Hand Jive." In the interim, he learned a lot more about music, starting with the uncle of a couple of neighborhood girls. On his way to a backyard party at the girls' house, he stopped to listen to the uncle practicing the trumpet. The uncle, who had been practicing scales, invited young John Veliotes in, and

> treated me to a little concert of riffs and melodies. The music he was playing was so different from the bottom line barrelhouse stuff we played with Count Otis Matthews' barrelhouse band. It was no less Black than what we did with the West Oakland House Rockers, and it contained flashes of pungent blues phrases, but there was a unique elegance here, an element of sophistication.
>
> What I was hearing was African American musical artistry lifted to its loftiest stage. In other words, so-called jazz. In later years, as I recruited players for my band, I remembered this man who possessed that critical balance between sophistication and heart . . . Without the rich African American culture, without the genuine, nurtured-in-the-south, pure Black blues feeling, jazz is empty, and to me, meaningless.

Musicians emigrated to Los Angeles. A first migration came in 1917, when the US Navy shut down the Storyville district of New Orleans, which sent Jelly Roll Morton, Kid Ory, and a host of other New Orleans musicians looking for new opportunities in the West. Later, in the 1920s and '30s. T-Bone Walker came from Texas, as did Camille Howard; Roy Milton was from Oklahoma. Charles Brown was a high school chemistry teacher in Texas and came to California as an apprentice electrician, before deciding to make a career in music. Joe and Jimmy Liggins were from Oklahoma, but their family moved to San Diego when they were in high school. They all found their way to Central Avenue: the Liggins brothers came up the coast, Johnny Otis down from the north, others from farther afield.

Still others were local, and although the East Coast didn't know it, Los Angeles had a strong musical core of its own. Hampton Hawes, Sonny Criss, and Big Jay McNeely all went to high school together and hung out together, studied together, and played together. Two of them would gravitate toward the new music of Charlie Parker, while the third—McNeely—would pick up the banner of Illinois Jacquet and become one of the most flamboyant honking tenormen of the new small-group swing.

McNeely describes some of his experiences growing up in Los Angeles:

> We had Eddie Davis. Buddy Collette and the Woodman Brothers and Charles Mingus, they all went to school with my brother, who was older. A lot of tenor players came from Watts. Like Walter Benton. He was a great saxophonist, man. He could play. Then you had Walter Henry . . . he was bad. Clifford Solomon. See, I used to go out and study, and then I'd come back and teach them. They wanted to learn, but they didn't have any money. They all used to come over to the house, and I'd give them instructions, lessons and things.[1]

McNeely studied with two prominent teachers in Los Angeles: Lloyd Reese, who taught Charles Mingus how to break down the music of Richard Strauss and Igor Stravinsky to its components, and Alma Hightower, whose students included Mingus, Jacquet, Hamilton, Dexter Gordon, Sonny Stitt, Melba Liston, and Roy Ayers. Classical music was an important part of the training of young Black musicians in Los Angeles in the 1930s and early '40s. Big Jay McNeely and Sonny Criss performed a Chopin waltz at their high school graduation ceremony. Charles Brown won amateur night at Central Avenue's Lincoln Theater by playing Earl Hines's boogie-woogie interpretation of "St. Louis Blues," then followed it up with an encore of movie composer Richard Addinsell's stirring tribute to the Allied cause, the *Warsaw Concerto*. Other young musicians in LA were students of Samuel Brown, who taught so many future jazz greats at Jefferson High School and frequently came to Central Avenue to cheer on his former acolytes. Les Hite's orchestra, one of the city's most prominent big bands, was almost all home-grown talent.

Figure 2.1. Lincoln Theater on Central Avenue today. CBI62, Creative Commons Attribution-Share Alike 3.0. Unported license.

The Lincoln Theater was a bellwether attraction on Central Avenue. The venerable Black newspaper the *California Eagle* called it "the finest and most beautiful theater in the country built exclusively for race patronage." Duke Ellington played there, as did Billie Holiday and Lionel Hampton, who was always guaranteed to bring the house down with "Flying Home." The Beacon Theater and the Elks Hall were also popular spots for headliner shows. The Club Alabam, where Johnny Otis led the house band, was a big attraction. Jimmy Witherspoon was a favorite at Lovejoy's. The Last Word, the Memo, Shepp's Playhouse, Jack's Basket, the Bird in the Basket, the Brown Bomber, the Nightcap were clubs and after-hours joints. West Coast bebop pioneer Howard McGhee held forth at the Down Beat.[2]

All of this made for a fecund cauldron in which new music could germinate and grow. The principal ingredients came from the streets, the schools, and the railroads, which brought in the newcomers from out of town. The street's music was made by people like Johnny Otis's Oakland buddy, Count Otis Matthews, which is hard to categorize from today's perspective. Otis describes it as "down home boogie woogie barrelhouse," and certainly it was characterized by youthful exuberance. Most likely, it was strongly influenced by early West Coast immigrant Jelly Roll Morton. And just as certainly, it was music to dance to, at backyard barbecues or impromptu street festivals.

Perhaps the key ingredient in the development of Central Avenue's jazz sound was the presence of the immigrants from the Southwest. Some, like Joe Turner and Pete Johnson, came from Kansas City, where a corrupt city government in the Prohibition era had created a wide-open environment in which music and musicians flourished. Others came from Texas and Oklahoma, where Kansas City–influenced territory bands were popular and influential during the 1920s and '30s.

The Great Migration of southern Blacks to northern cities often followed a vaguely geographical distribution, with those from the eastern seaboard states traveling to New York and Philadelphia, others from the Delta region coming to Chicago and Detroit, where the urban blues of Muddy Waters and John Lee Hooker took root, and from the Southwest to Los Angeles, particularly after 1942, when the Southern Pacific Railroad needed workers for its westernmost expansion, which facilitated the migration of hundreds of Black families.

One of the first important Southwestern musicians to make a name for himself in Los Angeles was Aaron Thibeaux "T-Bone" Walker, from Texas. Walker is one of the musicians Johnny Otis mentions as having "spanned the gap" between those of "technical ability and jazz sophistication" and those in the traditional blues field, making him an interesting anomaly. He had begun his career in Dallas, working as an apprentice to country blues performer Blind Lemon Jefferson. Jefferson was one of the most widely recorded blues singers of his era, and Walker's first recording, for Columbia in 1929, was that sort of guitar-and-vocal blues.

By 1935, Walker had assimilated himself into the Los Angeles scene, playing in Les Hite's orchestra. Hite had a big band that played at Sebastian's Cotton Club in Culver City (just outside the Los Angeles city limits and so not bound by that city's curfew laws) and at other clubs after Sebastian's shut down in 1938. Hite's band included, at various times, Lionel Hampton, Marshal Royal, Lawrence Brown, Britt Woodman, and Dizzy Gillespie. Walker recorded once with the band, in 1940, for Varsity Records, but only as a vocalist. The guitar part on "T-Bone Blues" is handled by Frank Pasley and is not prominent.

It was during this period that Walker began experimenting with an electric guitar, and he is credited, along with Charlie Christian and Les Paul, with being the first to do important work on that instrument. This is significant because as big band swing coalesced into the new small-group swing in the early 1940s, with two or three horns doing the work of an entire brass and woodwind section, the electric guitar became a much more important part of the sound; this was one of the ways in which the new swing differentiated itself from the old. Of course, this was much more true of the musicians like Muddy Waters, playing in what Johnny Otis called "the traditional blues field," which meant playing in loud clubs in urban industrial areas. Where the guitar was the lead instrument, they had to play loud to dominate the room. Bringing a guitar as a featured instrument into a jazz orchestra or small group required, as Otis points out, a different skill set and a different temperament.

Charlie Christian played with Benny Goodman, but his career was so short and his talent so unique, it took a while for his influence to be felt. T-Bone Walker's was more immediate, because he played such a prominent role in the Los Angeles jazz scene. And the Petrillo strike ensured that the West Coast small-group swing had a stealth development in the early 1940s. Walker made only one more recording session before the strike, on which he did play the guitar, with a band led by a white musician, pianist Freddie ("Beat Me Daddy, Eight to the Bar") Slack and his protégé, singer Ella Mae Morse. Like Nat "King" Cole, Walker was an active player on the scene but didn't go on to make other small-group swing records.

The sound which developed on Central Avenue, which was developed into the sound that would transform music in the 1940s and '50s, was the sound that combined the Chick Webb swing feeling of Louis Jordan, the arresting sound of Illinois Jacquet's honking tenor, and the driving shuffle variations on the blues of the Southwest territory bands. It developed in bands up and down Central Avenue, in anonymity beyond the confines of white Los Angeles, although not unheralded there. Veterans of the Central Avenue scene recall Humphrey Bogart, Ava Gardner, and other Hollywood royalty regularly checking out the scene.

Bardu Ali, like Louis Jordan a member of the Chick Webb orchestra, was reported to be the one who first recommended Ella Fitzgerald to Webb. He led the band for a short period after Webb's death, before Fitzgerald took it over. Ali decamped for the West Coast, where he led the house band at the Lincoln Theater, and employed both Charles Brown (after his Amateur Night victory) and Johnny Otis. Ali's band is one of those that had its heyday during the recording ban years, and his only credited appearance on record is one session in 1947 with the Johnny Otis band.

Johnny Otis was coming into his own in these years, with his first big break coming as leader of the band at the Club Alabam, located next to the Hotel Dunbar and a prime spot for Central Avenue jazz, which attracted both white and Black audiences. Some of the members of Otis's band included future jazz luminaries Curtis Counce, Paul Quinichette, Buddy Collette, Sonny Criss, and Hampton Hawes.

Otis's Club Alabam band is a pretty good snapshot of Central Avenue in the early 1940s. His band included musicians who were already excited by the new sounds and musicians who wanted to stay closer to the swing music they had grown up listening to but give it the new twist that was starting to happen. A good example of how that happened can be found in the stories of three high school friends: Hampton Hawes, Sonny Criss, and Big Jay McNeely.

Like everyone who was Black and wanted to play music, or just dance to music, they were drawn to Central Avenue. McNeely recalls:[3]

> I hit Central Avenue when I was a kid, man, because that was the thing in the forties . . . The Avenue was popping then. I was always on Central sneaking in. Young cats were getting in there to see what was going on . . . the Avenue was just on fire. You know what I mean?
>
> I was playing with Sonny Criss, Hampton Hawes—a great jazz pianist . . . at that time he used to sound like Nat King Cole. He used to love Nat. But we were very progressive . . . We followed Bird very closely. Howard McGhee, Diz, Miles Davis. See, they were all down on First Street. . . . We listened to the records . . . when the stuff was hot, we were right on top of it . . .
>
> Sonny had such a great ear that he could hear something once and play it. I didn't have the ability or the ear like he did to hear something and to play it as fast. I'm kind of glad, because I was able to develop and create my own style.
>
> When we got out of school, that's when each one began to go his own direction. Fortunately, I found where I belonged in this stream of music, and Sonny had his thing, and Hamp did. So they stayed in the progressive thing. But periodically we

would cross paths. We'd laugh, we'd talk, and we'd have a good time. So they respected me, because they knew what I could do, what I was capable of doing, and what I felt about music. The showmanship was one thing, playing is another thing.

McNeely's direction included serious study with Joseph Cadaly, first saxophone chair with the RKO Studio Orchestra. He studied theory, harmony, and composition with Cadaly, who also "taught me all about full vibrato, so I could play with a big sound . . . you have to have the proper approach. You have to use your whole body as a soundboard. My sax began to sound as smooth as a cello when I studied with him." That big sound was to stand him in good stead in his professional career. His time on Central Avenue included forging a friendship with Charlie Parker—McNeely's mother used to wash Parker's clothes for him—but Lester Young and Illinois Jacquet were his chief influences. And his gift for showmanship developed not in the show biz capital of the world, but nearly a continent away, in the little town of Clarksville, Tennessee, a stop on a series of one-nighters. As he told Marc Myers in an interview:

> When we played Clarksville for the first time, the audience didn't respond. They just sat there. I couldn't understand that. The music usually got people going. So on the next set I did something different. I got down on my knees to play. Then I laid down on the stage and played from there . . . People went crazy. After the concert, I said to myself, "I'm going to try this again." So I did it in Texas. And again, everyone went crazy. Back in L.A., I did it, too. The kids went nuts. They loved that I was on my back blowing like that, and my energy fired up theirs.

McNeely was arguably the most controversial of Jacquet's followers, because he took what Jacquet had begun and pushed it to the furthest extreme. "Every time we picked up our horns we were just elaborating on that," he once said, referring to Jacquet's "Flying Home" solo, "Trying to make it bigger, wilder, give it more swing, more kick." As with many of the Jacquet school, McNeely downplayed his credentials as a jazz musician. But he was a featured performer in two Los Angeles Cavalcade of Jazz shows.

McNeely, schooled in music with the best teachers Los Angeles had to offer, had to learn to loosen up, get funky, play a more populist form of music. He, like other musicians brought up in the urban sophistication of the California metropolis, would learn a lot from the new arrivals, immigrants from the Southwest and its territory bands. One such was Roy Milton.

As a teenager in Oklahoma, Milton had joined Ernie Fields's band as a singer. One night, at a gig on the road, the band suddenly found itself without a drummer. There was no one else, so young Roy sat in behind the drum kit; he never left. Working in Fields's band was a great apprenticeship for Milton. It was one of the best-known territory bands, popular with white and Black audiences alike—so much so that Bob Wills, the king of Western swing, used his influence to make Fields's band the first Black ensemble to play at Tulsa's legendary Cain's Ballroom.

Milton emigrated to Los Angeles in 1935 and arrived with the experience and ambition to begin to make a name for himself on Central Avenue. He started his own band in 1937, at a club called Louis' Café, on Pico Boulevard, just off Central. This was still very much the big band era, but Milton, like others in his situation, was finding that he had to compete using what he could manage, which was two horns and a piano. The horns were a trumpet player and a reed man who doubled on clarinet and saxophone, giving the band a little more variety in its sound. As the '30s turned into the '40s, there would be less demand for a clarinet. His piano player was a woman, Betty Hall Jones, which was unusual for the time; she had come from Kansas City, where she had played with Buster Moten, and added her brand of Kansas City swing to the mix. She would go on to have a substantial career as a musician and composer, with songs recorded by Ray Charles and Nellie Lutcher.

Jones made enough of an impression on Milton that when he came to put together a trio in 1943, as Nat "King" Cole's sound became the rage, he hired another woman—the great Camille Howard—who would be with him for many years. Howard would anchor Milton's eventual six-piece band, Roy Milton's Solid Senders, who would be rehearsed and battle-tested and ready when record-making began to happen again, and independent record labels sprang up to meet the demand for the new small-group swing by Black artists.

Equally important in bringing the gritty Southwestern sound to Central Avenue's mix was Milton's fellow Oklahoman Joe Liggins. They were often asked later in life if they had known each other back in Oklahoma, but Milton was from the relatively metropolitan Tulsa, and Liggins was born, and spent his early years, in the tiny town of Seminole, ninety miles away. He grew up listening to the territory bands and the Black church music of rural Oklahoma, but he never played in those bands. In

1932, when he was fifteen, his family moved to San Diego. He graduated from high school there, attended San Diego State College, played in local bands, and came to Los Angeles in 1939, where he joined a band called Sammy Franklin's California Rhythm Rascals. The Rhythm Rascals played for dancing, accompanying all the latest dance crazes. In 1942, they were confronted with a new one called the Texas Hop. Everyone wanted to do the Texas Hop, and there was nothing in the band's repertoire that quite fit, so Liggins wrote an instrumental number that would fit it.

It was an idea he had been fooling around with for a while, and its genesis, improbably, came from Art Tatum's improvisations on "Lady Be Good." As Liggins told Dick Lillard of Washington, DC, radio station WOL, he started with a sound he had picked up in the holiness churches for which he played the piano starting at age nine: "They had this pronounced beat on two and four and it gets to be a part of you if you play it long enough as I did for eight years." The beat stayed with him one day at the piano:

> I was fooling around on the piano with a tune called "Lady Be Good," and what I was trying to do was a little imitation of Art Tatum who had done "Lady Be Good," and he had this hard beat on the left hand and he can do some really wild stuff, man. It sounded like he had three hands. He had this hard beat in his left hand along with a regular bass and I'm trying to get this thing going and improvise "Lady Be Good" on the right hand.
>
> Now, I knew I wasn't playing "Lady Be Good"—I was playing something else, but it sounded good, so I kept it in. I kept working on this thing and finally about a month, a month and a half, I came up with all the music for "The Honeydripper."

He first called the piece "Cripple Joe," in tribute to an injury he'd suffered playing baseball, but soon found the new title and the perfect tune for the Texas Hop. During those strike years when recording was suspended, there was only one way for a song to become a hit, and that was word of mouth. "The Honeydripper" got it, and the Samba Club, where the Rascals were playing, became one of the hottest spots in town, as people came to hear that new song and do that new dance. Liggins had three years to perfect "The Honeydripper," as the new small-group swing of Central Avenue continued to percolate, unnoticed. That was about to change, as 1945 rolled around.

CHAPTER THREE

A New Sound

Joe Liggins has often told the story of how "The Honeydripper" was scouted. Leon René had parlayed his success in composing the hit song "When the Swallows Come Back to Capistrano" into starting an independent record company, Exclusive Records. He had heard about this song everyone was talking about, and dancing to, and he came down to the Samba Club, where the band was playing, to see for himself. By this time, "The Honeydripper" was enough of a draw that Sammy Franklin's Rhythm Rascals had decided to make it the evening's show-stopping tune. Music curfew for the clubs at that time was midnight, so "The Honeydripper" was played at quarter to twelve.

René arrived early, went up to Liggins at the piano, and requested the song.

"We don't play it till quarter to twelve," he was told.

René protested. He was a busy man, he couldn't stay that long. "Quarter to twelve." That was it; it wasn't going to be changed. So René stayed.

Afterward, he came up to Liggins again, and thanked him. It was worth the wait; he had not only heard everyone's favorite song, but so much more great original music. Who writes it? He wondered.

"I do," Liggins replied.

Liggins was all ready to record the song with the Rhythm Rascals, but there was a hitch. Mrs. Sammy Franklin was not about to let the band record anything but her husband's songs. So Liggins gave notice and started his own band: Joe Liggins and His Honeydrippers.

Leon René, and his brother Otis, who formed Excelsior Records, were part of a vanguard that was to reshape American music: the small

Figure 3.1. "The Honeydripper" original record label. Public domain.

independent record label. This was a business that was possible in ways that it had never been before. World War II's military production demands had lit a fire under American manufacturing, and now a lot of factories were retooling to meet the demands of a postwar consumer economy. The pressing of phonograph records had once only been available to the major labels; now anyone could get a record pressed. The René brothers were even able to set up their own pressing plant.[1] New technology had also made the recording process easier and cheaper.

And equally important, there was an untapped market. As Nelson George says in *The Death of Rhythm and Blues*: "For the masses of blacks, after bebop's emergence, jazz was respected, but in times of leisure and relaxation they turned to Louis Jordan and a blend of blues, jump blues, ballads, gospel, and a slew of sax-led instruments and fading black swing orchestras."

George is accepting the narrow definition of "jazz" that gained currency in the 1940s, perhaps narrowing it even further, as he seems to be placing the "fading black swing orchestras" of bandleaders like Erskine

Hawkins and Jimmie Lunceford, along with the "slew of sax-led instruments" that presumably are the new small-group swing combos (including Louis Jordan), along with blues and ballads, two perennial staples of jazz, outside looking in. But he's right about the music: it was what Blacks were listening to, and they weren't finding it on records. The major labels were recording Duke Ellington and Count Basie, the Ink Spots, and the newly anointed Nat "King" Cole (on the fledgling major label Capitol) but not much else in the way of Black artists.

The new independent labels did not have the budget or the studio space to handle the Duke Ellington orchestra or even the Jimmie Lunceford orchestra, but they could handle a small group like Joe Liggins and His Honeydrippers. They did not have the national distribution network of a major label, but with their shoestring budgets, they did not need to match the sales of a Glenn Miller, Jo Stafford, or Frank Sinatra to make a living off what they were doing.

Liggins formed his new group in partnership with his close friend from childhood, Little Willie Jackson, on alto and baritone saxophones. Jackson, blind from birth, was limited as to the stage acrobatics he could perform. Perhaps because of this, he would never branch out on his own, like Illinois Jacquet or Big Jay McNeely, but stayed with Liggins throughout his career. Red Callender played bass on the Exclusive Records sessions; Frank Pasley, of Les Hite's orchestra, was on guitar. James Jackson was on tenor sax and would continue with Liggins into the 1950s, recording also with Blue Lu Barker and Percy Mayfield. Peppy Prince, who had been with Les Hite, was on drums.

They went into the René brothers' studio in April 1945 to record a few sides with crooner Herb Jeffries, and a few other tunes on their own, but mostly to record "The Honeydripper." Leon René was hedging his bets here. He had signed up Liggins and his band primarily on the strength of his audience-pleasing, foot-stomping "Honeydripper," but he wasn't quite willing to go all in right away. He was going to start with his small-group swing ensemble playing a new version of the swing that audiences were used to hearing before he hit them with an altogether new type of swing. Jeffries had recorded with Earl Hines and Duke Ellington. He would go on to a markedly different career—producing a series of low-budget, all-Black Westerns starring himself as a singing cowboy. He had that familiar baritone, reminiscent of Billy Eckstine. He sang two songs, "I Left a Good Deal in Mobile," which would be the A side of the record, and "Here's Hoping."

The second day in the studio was just the band, with no singer, and they started out with a swing tune, another Liggins composition that René had presumably heard and liked at the Samba Club, called "Blue Moods," in the sweet swing style one associates with the Dorsey Brothers, but bluesier. Then they were ready to let go. René warned them to keep it under three minutes, to make it fit on a 78 RPM record. Liggins was used to jamming on the tune for at least fifteen minutes, bringing down the house with it, and he protested that they couldn't do it justice in so short a time. They finally agreed to do it as a two-sided record, at just over six minutes.

If long-playing technology had been invented about five years earlier, they could have done a whole fifteen minute jam on one side of a ten-inch LP, and I wonder if it would have become the phenomenon it became. Three minutes per side put it onto the jukeboxes, and a lot of people, especially younger people who couldn't get into nightclubs, were dancing to those jukeboxes.

Leon René certainly seems to have realized what he had. "The Honeydripper" became his first Liggins release. It was Exclusive Records' catalog #207. "I Left a Good Deal in Mobile" followed it at #208, and "Blue Moods" was #210. It became an instant sensation on *Billboard*'s Race Records chart, zooming up to number one, where it stayed for eighteen weeks—twenty-seven weeks on the list altogether. *Billboard* had recently changed the name of its chart from Harlem Hit Parade—just in time, as it turned out, since "The Honeydripper" served notice that Harlem was no longer the center of the musical universe.

Liggins was from Oklahoma, but he and Texan Little Willie Jackson had gone to high school in San Diego, where they were able to take advantage of the music education programs that California schools had to offer. He had been playing and taking lessons since he was eight, and certainly, like every piano player in Los Angeles, he had heard and admired Nat "King" Cole. But for "The Honeydripper" he elected to go for a more basic, primitive sound, reminiscent of the boogie-woogie of Jimmy Yancey, along with some of the pulsing beats that Jelly Roll Morton and other piano players had brought from New Orleans and that Pete Johnson had brought from Kansas City. Little Willie Jackson and James Jackson (not related) have a sound that comes out of the territory band saxophonists like Buster Smith, with the by-now obligatory influence of Illinois Jacquet, but it's also interesting to note how much the vibrato-laden sax stars of the swing era, like Jimmy Dorsey, influenced Little Willie's playing, especially

Figure 3.2. Jimmie Lunceford, New York, ca. August 1946. William P. Gottlieb Collection, Library of Congress, Music Division.

on a tune like "Blue Moods." The unison singing of the riff-based melody is a device that Nat Cole employed on some of his early recordings.

"The Honeydripper" has entered the jazz repertoire sufficiently over the years to have gained the status of at least a quasi-standard. Cab Calloway and Jimmie Lunceford were the first to record cover versions of it. Lunceford's version, on Decca, employed the Delta Rhythm Boys for the vocal, giving that part of the recording more attention than Liggins had on the original. Other 1945 recordings included blues singer/pianist Roosevelt Sykes (given that he was nicknamed "The Honeydripper," he could hardly have passed it up), Bull Moose Jackson, and Maxwell Davis. Sammy Franklin, a little late to the party, decided to record "The Honeydripper," but no one was listening. The following year, Cootie Williams, Earl Hines, and Oscar Peterson would add their versions, and as the decade ended, it was taken up by German swing bandleader Max Greger and Tommy

Dorsey's group-within-a-group, the Clambake Seven. This was not quite the all-star Seven that Dorsey had in the mid-'30s, but it did include Billy Butterfield and Peanuts Hucko. Over the decades, "The Honeydripper" would be revived by a number of jazz artists, including King Curtis, Count Basie with Joe Turner, Herbie Mann, and Brother Jack McDuff.

In addition to recording the tune, Lunceford also hired Liggins as an arranger for several other sessions. He was one of the featured musicians at the first five presentations of the Cavalcade of Jazz, an ongoing series of jazz festivals held in Los Angeles from 1945 to 1958. It was one of the most important jazz festivals of its day and the first major festival ever to be organized by an African American. The organizer was entrepreneur Leon Hefflin Sr., and he did not shy away from the Black musical artists of Central Avenue.

This was a time, and a place, when music was more fluid. The strict definitions of jazz that were being drawn up in *DownBeat* and *Metronome* were not being applied on Central Avenue. Liggins kept the same basic lineup of musicians he had started out with, but his recordings also included jazz figures like Callender, Johnny Moore of Johnny Moore's Three Blazers, and New Orleans clarinetist Joe Darensbourg.

And when you think of it, the genesis of "The Honeydripper" is not so different from what Liggins's more advanced contemporaries were doing—creating an improvisation which became a new tune, on the framework of an earlier standard. Liggins started listening to Tatum's recording of "Lady Be Good," tried to play it, found himself unable to duplicate Tatum's left hand because nobody could, substituted the left-hand rhythms from his church background, improvised from there, and gradually arrived at "The Honeydripper."

Small-group swing was happening in other parts of the country, too, in response to the same economic phenomenon: the difficulty of sustaining a big band, and the proliferation of small independent labels that were open to recording small combos that also could see the possibilities of marketing to an emerging urban Black audience.

Wynonie Harris, originally a Midwesterner, spent some formative time on Central Avenue but did not stay there. Originally from Omaha, Nebraska, he began singing in clubs in his hometown, then was drawn, as so many Midwesterners were, to Kansas City. There, Harris listened to and learned from blues singers like Big Joe Turner—who frequently partnered with boogie-woogie pianist Pete Johnson—and Jimmy Rushing, vocalist with Kansas City's top jazz ensembles, Walter Page's Blue Devils and Bennie Moten's band. Next he made his way out to Los Angeles in 1940 and found work at the Club Alabam, then one of the hottest clubs on Central Avenue, where he started to build a reputation. But he soon moved on, to Chicago, where he caught the attention of bandleader Lucky Millinder.

Millinder took him to New York and his first recording session. Millinder successfully swam against the tide, keeping a big band going throughout the decade. He was an interesting story. He played no instruments, sang rarely, and had no particular gifts as a composer or arranger, but he knew how to put a band together, and keep it together, playing sweet swing in the late 1930s and early 1940s, shifting more in the direction of the sound that came to be identified as rhythm and blues as the decade went on. Musicians who played in his band over the years included Dizzy Gillespie, Don Byas, Bill Doggett, Sam "the Man" Taylor, Bull Moose Jackson, Danny Barker, Tyree Glenn—the cream of New Orleans style, swing, bebop, and small-group swing.

Millinder's shift from the sweet swing sound to the more hard driving sound came on May 25, 1944, when he went into a New York studio with Harris replacing suave crooner Trevor Bacon. The band recorded six songs that day, two of them featuring Harris on vocals. One of those was "Who Threw the Whiskey in the Well?" With a hard-driving swing arrangement, rhythm propelled by church-style handclapping along with Panama Francis's drumming, and a "congregation" backing him up on vocals, Harris delivered Deacon Jones's sermon on the evils of lacing the parish's well with whiskey. Released on June 9, 1945, it shot up to number one on the *Billboard* Race Records charts and stayed there for eight weeks, with twenty weeks on the charts altogether. The song was Millinder's biggest hit, but it is mostly remembered today as a Wynonie Harris record. Harris showed, on his debut recording, a rare melodic sophistication for someone who came to be known as a "blues shouter." He had learned to work in the jazz style by listening to how Jimmy Rushing handled it; Rushing also made his reputation as a blues shouter, but he always thought of himself as a ballad singer.

Not long after the release of the record, while they were touring the Southwest, Harris parted company with Millinder, after a dispute over money; Harris thought he was worth more, Millinder disagreed. Harris turned out to be right, because the promoter for their next gig at a venue in Houston canceled the booking when he heard that Harris had left the band. Millinder convinced Harris to come back (for a substantial raise), but that was their last show together. Bull Moose Jackson took over the vocal chores with the band, and Harris headed back for Central Avenue.

Harris cut a record in the summer of 1945 with one of the new independent labels out of LA. It was then called Philo but was soon to be better known as Aladdin. He worked with a band put together by his old friend from the Club Alabam, Johnny Otis. He followed it up a short time later, on August 2, 1945, with a band led by Illinois Jacquet.

Harris was a singer, and his records after "Who Threw the Whiskey in the Well?" came out under his name, with the name of the bandleader included on the label, but not the rest of the personnel, as was frequently done with small-group jazz records.

The question of what makes a jazz singer has been often debated. I'll offer a simple definition of my own: a jazz singer is someone who can sing with jazz musicians and not get lost, and who can add something to the sound. Later in this book, we'll discuss jazz musicians who have added an improvised, swinging interlude to recordings by non-jazz singers, but in this time, the mid-1940s, swing was still at the forefront of musicians' minds, either to break from it (the beboppers), to keep playing it (Jimmie Lunceford, Benny Goodman, Harry James), or to adapt it to a small-group setting and a more modern beat.

Wynonie Harris was certainly focusing on the small-group swing style. His first session with Otis's band included "Around the Clock Blues" (parts 1 and 2), "Cock a Doodle Doo," and "Yonder Goes My Baby." What was the music like? "Around the Clock," with the Otis ensemble, is no relation to the later Louis Jordan–inspired rock and roll hit by Bill Haley, "Rock Around the Clock." It has some wonderful percussive piano playing by pianist Lee Wesley Jones, a swinging ensemble head by the front men McGhee and Edwards, and solos by all three that are worth listening to. Harris belts a basic blues lyric—one that was adopted more or less whole by Chuck Berry for "Reelin' and Rockin'" and sampled by Arthur "Big Boy" Crudup for "So Glad You're Mine" (later covered by Elvis Presley). This is part of the reason why Harris is so frequently mentioned as a godfather of rock and roll, as if being a harbinger of rock and roll were the most important thing you could say about the new music of the 1940s.

Edwards sits out "Cock a Doodle Doo," but McGhee and Jones more than make up for his absence. McGhee is probably best known as one of the early beboppers, but he shows here that he can swing the blues. There's little of the Jacquet-style ecstatic blowing here, but plenty of blues and plenty of jazz. Harris, especially on "Cock a Doodle Doo," brings an ecstatic element, which he will build on in later recordings.

"Around the Clock" began to draw serious attention to Harris as a performer on his own, but "Wynonie's Blues," with Jacquet, released on the New York independent label Apollo, was his breakout hit. It went to number three on the *Billboard* chart. Harris definitely establishes himself as a hitmaking singer on this cut, but Jacquet matches him. Unlike the Otis band's recordings, which feature a succession of soloists, in the style of most small-group jazz, there are two principal voices here: Harris and Jacquet, working off each other.

Harris continued to record in Los Angeles, including with groups led by Oscar Pettiford and Jack McVea. He also recorded the Lionel Hampton hit, "Hey-ba-ba-rebop," with a group called the Hamp-Tone Allstars, for the Hamp-Tone label, founded by Lionel's wife Gladys. The label was a home, for its brief existence, to small-group swing, as demonstrated by the musicians on this session, including Joe Morris and Ernie Fields. Hitting the road, Harris stopped to make a record on May 14, 1946, in Nashville with a four-piece that may have included Harris himself on drums. Of particular interest there is "Dig This Boogie," a track featuring just drums, vocals, and driving boogie-woogie piano played by Herman "Sonny" Blount, who would become better known as Sun Ra. In New York, Harris surrounded himself with many of the best musicians in town, including Joe Newman, Tab Smith, Allen Eager, Bill Doggett, and a wonderful guitar player who has faded into obscurity after an A-list career, Mary Osborne. In 1947 he recorded a duet session with Big Joe Turner.

November 1947 found Harris in the studios of King Records in Cincinnati, where he recorded his next number one hit, with a group led by trumpeter "Hot Lips" Page. The song, "Good Rockin' Tonight," was his biggest hit, and it continues to be considered something of a landmark, but again as a precursor to rock and roll. It deserves to be appreciated for what it was in its own time, a time when rock and roll did not exist, white teenagers were not part of the audience, and mature Black audiences were dancing to jazz with a beat, played by musicians who knew their music and their audience.

Oran "Hot Lips" Page, originally from Texas, came to Kansas City in the Prohibition era, as so many territory musicians did. He played with Walter Page's (no relation) Blue Devils, Bennie Moten, and Count Basie. He came to New York in the mid-1930s, where he soon became ubiquitous,

Figure 3.3. "Hot Lips" Page, Apollo Theater, New York, ca. October 1946. William P. Gottlieb Collection, Library of Congress, Music Division.

playing after-hours sessions in many Harlem clubs, including Minton's Playhouse; going on the road with Artie Shaw and Bud Freeman; and recording with nearly everyone, from proto-bebop to neo-Dixieland, with Eddie Condon, and with a band led by Mezz Mezzrow and Sidney Bechet.

King was one of the most interesting independent labels of the 1940s, not least for its location away from the major music centers of New York, Los Angeles, and Chicago. It had been founded by local entrepreneur Syd Nathan in 1943 to record hillbilly music, as it was called then. When Lucky Millinder's orchestra came to town, Nathan had already started thinking about branching out into other areas. He found the perfect associate in Millinder's trumpet player/arranger Henry Glover. Glover decided to stay on in Cincinnati and take the job as A&R director for his race division. Glover turned out to have a talent for producing country music as well and soon took over the production duties for the whole operation.

King's race records line featured a number of significant leaders of small-group swing ensembles, including Tiny Bradshaw and Earl Bostic. And King's Tiny Bradshaw Orchestra, a six-piece band, was augmented by Hot Lips Page in late November accompanying Big Maybelle. The key players in that Bradshaw band were two tenor sax players, Hal Singer, who was to become one of the important small-group swing bandleaders in a few years, and Tom Archia, who had made a mark in Los Angeles with both Howard McGhee/Teddy Edwards and the Jacquet brothers. Guitarist Lonnie Johnson was also on the session, as was drummer Bobby Donaldson, who continued to be a much-in-demand session man through the next three decades. The same core became the Hot Lips Page Orchestra a week or so later, when they backed up Lonnie Johnson, Marion Abernathy, and then Big Maybelle again.

The musicians show their range on these sessions. Big Maybelle's "Indian Giver" has a soft but emotive setting, suggestive of 1930s swing; "Bad Dream Blues" has a trumpet-vocal dialog that hearkens back to Bessie Smith's work with Louis Armstrong or Joe Smith, plus an electric guitar solo by Johnson that has the technical skill of T-Bone Walker. Marion Abernathy's "My Man Boogie" is classic small-group swing, with a solid groove underlaid by Earl Knight's boogie-woogie piano and an exuberant, imaginative solo by Page.

Page and his group participated in two sessions in King's studios on December 23 and 28, 1943, backing several vocalists, including Wynonie Harris on a total of eleven songs. The second session yielded what proved to be the most successful song, "Good Rockin' Tonight." "Good Rockin' Tonight" has a gospel feel, with the rhythm supplied by handclaps and an intro by Page that suggests "When the Saints Go Marchin' In." It's not the overt gospel style that Ray Charles would introduce later, but it has the exuberance, in the handclaps, Harris's vocal, and the instrumental breaks, to get its audience up and dancing.

Harris's career continued strong into the early 1950s, and he often drew on a stable of jazz accompanists, including such musicians as Cat Anderson, Frank "Floorshow" Culley, Connie Kay, Johnny Griffin, Joe Morris, Elmo Hope, Gene Ramey, Curtis Peagler, Milt Buckner, Big John Greer, Tyree Glenn, Rudy Powell, and Buddy Lucas.

Los Angeles continued to be the most important breeding ground for this new sound. Another Southwesterner who found his way to Central Avenue was Roy Milton—like Joe Liggins, from Oklahoma. Milton told

Johnny Otis in an interview: "I was in the city, he was in the country. I didn't know [him] until I came out here in California. I left Oklahoma in '35. I don't know if Joe was already here then or not. First I heard of him was when he got a band organized and that was in the '40s. We used to play a lot of his numbers—'Honeydripper,' 'Pink Champagne.'" Milton and his group, the Solid Senders, became one of the most popular groups on Central Avenue. He was one of the first musicians signed by music entrepreneur Art Rupe, and he recorded his first hit, "R. M. Blues," for Rupe's short-lived independent label, Juke Box Records. It stayed on the charts for twenty-five weeks, rising as high as number two, right underneath Lionel Hampton, then Louis Jordan, and then Jordan with Ella Fitzgerald. Rupe then founded a new label, Specialty, which was destined to become the most important of the LA-based independents, and Milton went with him.

A characteristic of much of the early small-group swing records was how closely, in many ways, it resembled big band swing, with its emphasis on arrangements and an ensemble sound. The genius of the small-group arrangers, starting with Louis Jordan, was that they were able to get that ensemble sound with only a few instruments. At least at the beginning, they somewhat overlooked the lesson of the beboppers, who realized that one of the advantages of a small group was that it could give extended time to virtuoso performances by soloists of distinctive ability.

Milton's Solid Senders had a such a musician right from the start, the pianist Camille Howard. Another Southwesterner, she moved to Los Angeles in the early 1940s and almost immediately clicked with Milton, who was forming a piano trio, then stayed with him as he formed his swing group and began recording. As a drummer, Milton was one of the first to add a back beat to a boogie-woogie rhythm, making it irresistible for dancing; for that innovation, he is frequently cited as a significant precursor to rock and roll. But listening to his records today, what really stands out and lifts them above so many of his contemporaries on this burgeoning scene is Howard's rock-solid, yet feather-light boogie-woogie piano and her improvisations on the basic boogie riffs. She would go on to become an outstanding featured performer in her own right, then retired from the commercial music scene because of religious convictions, but her tenure with Milton was a rich one.

Howard would record under her own name, in addition to her work with Milton. Her "X-Temporaneous Boogie," recorded on December 31,

1947, is an acknowledged masterpiece of the genre, blending boogie-woogie with modernism.

"R. M. Blues" was Milton's biggest hit, but he continued to record for Specialty, and to have chart success, through the early 1950s. He added a second strong soloist in late 1946 when alto saxophonist Caughey Roberts joined the band. Roberts had played with Louis Armstrong (in the 1936 film *Pennies from Heaven*), with Fats Waller, and with Count Basie from 1937 to 1942 (including a performance in another feature film, *Reveille with Beverly*). Roberts remained with Milton through the end of 1947; when he left, he was replaced by Los Angeles native Jackie Kelso, once his student, who was now outshining the master. Reminiscing about the two most important band associations of his career, in *Central Avenue Sounds*, Kelso said: "When I played with Lionel Hampton, I played one way; when I played with Roy Milton, a totally different way. Both of them equally authentic, both of them equally real." Tenor saxophonist Benny Waters, who had played with King Oliver, Fletcher Henderson, Claude Hopkins, and Jimmie Lunceford, joined the band at around the same time as Kelso.

So why, with this lineup of talent, was Milton's music not recognized and embraced by the jazz establishment? Again, it fell outside of the narrative. Small-group swing, largely though not entirely born in California, came from the music that was brought into California from New Orleans and the Southwest, and from Kansas City and the territory bands with their strong Kansas City influence. The tunes these musicians played were mostly blues and blues-influenced.

The two other principal jazz styles of the period, bebop and swing, mostly came from the North, from New York and Chicago. In many important ways, these were stylistic opposites and certainly cultural opposites. Big band swing, as it developed through the 1930s, was primarily a white music, and bebop, although some important white musicians were on board with it from early days, developed out of Black consciousness. But both of these musical styles leaned heavily on the work of white composers like George Gershwin and Jerome Kern, utilizing more elaborate chord structures. The white musicians did so because it was the popular music they'd grown up with, the Black musicians largely because the more intricate chord structures gave them a basis for the intellectually challenging music that they were drawn to.

These challenges were not limited by American popular song, as Igor Stravinsky discovered when he went to hear Charlie Parker play at Birdland.

Informed that Stravinsky was in the house, Parker pretended not to notice, not even glancing in the famed modernist composer's direction. Instead, he took the band into "Koko," one of the most technically challenging pieces in his repertoire, and, as he came to the second chorus, deftly interposed the opening of Stravinsky's *Firebird Suite* into his improvisation. Stravinsky became a fan for life, and the moment became not only a part of Parker's legend, but a part of the legend of bebop.

It was an era when lines were drawn between high culture and mass culture, in music and in other art forms. Walt Whitman had sunk into obscurity because the literary critics of the day, caught up in dissecting types of ambiguity, could find nothing to analyze in his work.

Charlie Parker was not one to draw those exclusionary lines. He had a deep and passionate connection to the blues. In Clint Eastwood's movie *Bird*, there's a scene in which Parker is aghast at hearing a rival playing rhythm and blues. Critics found many things to hate in Eastwood's movie, but that scene wasn't one of them. Yet it was one of the movie's more unrealistic scenes. In real life, Parker did not live in a rarefied world in which Stravinsky was in and rhythm and blues was out.

Parker didn't, and musicians in general didn't, but the people who wrote about music and the promoters who presented music were a different story. And here, race played a role. The critics, concert promoters, and club owners who presented jazz were keenly aware of the central role played by Black artists in the development of the music, and they were also keenly aware of the evils of segregation. They took a courageous stand against the egregious practices of racism that had to be addressed in that time, but a closer examination of the subtle and pervasive nature of racism as the warp and woof of American society would have to wait for another era. In the early 1940s, the proponents of jazz as an American art form knew enough to seek out Minton's Playhouse as opposed to the Cotton Club or Connie's Inn. But there was another stratum they were not reaching.

I was there. Not in the 1940s but in a time not so different. In 1958, as an eighteen-year-old kid, having newly discovered jazz, I went to Small's Paradise on 135th Street and 7th Avenue in Harlem. I honestly don't remember whether I was the only white person there in the audience, but I certainly wasn't the only white person there. Pepper Adams was on the bandstand, along with Donald Byrd. Now, I didn't go there because I knew a white guy would be playing. I probably didn't even know Pepper Adams was white when I decided to go there. The music was fantastic. I felt like I was where I belonged, in the world of jazz, which was just opening up to me. But when I left Small's, I walked down 7th to 133rd Street and there was a small club called Count Basie's. I went in, but I didn't stay. I don't know why not. Maybe because I was disappointed not to find Count Basie there. Maybe because I didn't know who was playing, and I didn't trust my own ears enough to know whether music played by musicians I'd never heard of was any good. But I think there was a barrier. I think I felt like I didn't belong.

Someone who may have broken through that barrier, oddly enough because one tends to think of his later recordings of artists who had huge white followings, was Norman Granz. He did go to Central Avenue, but that in itself was no big deal. Lots of whites, including movie stars, went to Central Avenue. But he also organized jam sessions that brought the Central Avenue musicians together, from Nat Cole to Charles Mingus to Big Jay McNeely.

His Jazz at the Philharmonic concerts, which were to grow into an international phenomenon, began as a benefit for a defense fund for some Hispanic kids who had been arrested during the notorious "zoot suit riot."

The concert, initially billed as "A Jazz Concert at the Philharmonic Auditorium," was such a success that, with its shortened name, it became a regular event, first in Los Angeles and then across the country. It featured stars like Charlie Parker and Lester Young, and it always featured the crowd-pleasing Illinois Jacquet, even though the jazz critical establishment generally put down Jacquet for his onstage flamboyance, both musically ("his name should be spelled 'Illinoise'") and theatrically—essentially for his Blackness. Jacquet was critiqued for his performance, a performance geared toward his Black audience.

CHAPTER FOUR

Postwar Explosion

After the war, Central Avenue was the home to a lot more than just the hard-driving small groups. Visiting jazz musicians like Charlie Parker gravitated there. Lester Young spent some time there playing in a group with his brother Lee. Nat "King" Cole was there all the time until his big breakthrough, and his talent and charisma made him an influential figure.

The musicians who followed in Cole's footsteps mostly sacrificed a little of his musical sophistication while adding a little blues. The first one to parlay this combination into success was a thirty-one-year-old GI named Cecil Gant. He had had a small but successful career in Nashville before wartime service in the army brought him to Los Angeles, where he appeared in uniform playing piano at a war bonds rally. Gant caused enough of a stir that he found himself in demand at war bond rallies all over the city and before long signed to Gilt Edge Records.

Gilt Edge was one of the odder stories in the history of wartime and postwar independent record labels. Founded by Arkansas transplant "Arkie" Shibley, it mostly issued country and western records by Shibley and others, but also slipped in a couple of jazz releases by Teddy Bunn, Big Jim Wynn, and Wingy Manone. In Cecil Gant—trading on his war bond rally success, he performed in uniform and was billed as Pvt. Cecil Gant—they had their only bona fide hitmaker. Gant's first recording session for Gilt Edge produced "Cecil's Boogie," a lively boogie-woogie piano number, and a vocal, "I Wonder," done in the blues-meets-Nat "King" Cole style.

Gilt Edge was a little ahead of the game. The war was still going on, which meant that shellac was still a national defense priority, but they managed to get records pressed. "I Wonder" became a hit, regarded by many as the first rhythm and blues recording. "I Wonder" was covered by both Louis Prima, with a big band swing arrangement, and Louis Armstrong. It has since been recorded by Dakota Staton, Ray Charles, and Etta Jones, with instrumental versions by Si Zentner and Gene Ammons. It was Gant's only breakout hit, but he continued to record with some success—ballads, up-tempo jive numbers, and boogie-woogie piano—until his death of pneumonia in 1951.

Although Gant was the first to record in this style, Cole's influence had been felt in Los Angeles for some time, most notably by his old South Central flatmate, Charles Brown. The Nat "King" Cole Trio featured jazz guitarist Oscar Moore, and Moore's younger brother Johnny had formed a trio of his own, Johnny Moore's Three Blazers. modeled along the same lines. On Cole's recommendation, when the Blazers lost their original pianist, Moore hired Brown. When the independent Atlas record label lost Cole to Capitol Records and megastardom, it signed Oscar Moore's younger brother to take his place. Unfortunately, with Atlas Johnny was still the kid brother—the group was billed as Oscar Moore and the Three Blazers, so Johnny and his trio moved on.

The Blazers backed up a protégé of Cole's and Brown's who used to hang around their South Central flat absorbing a musical education: the white singer Frankie Laine. They then recorded for Leon René's Exclusive label, with Brown on piano but not as vocalist. This time the vocal chores were given to another singer/pianist in the blues-Cole amalgam style, Ivory Joe Hunter, who would go on to a solo career of his own.

Finally, on September 11, 1945, recording for Philo/Aladdin, they came up with the song that brought the trio, and particularly Brown, now their singer-pianist, into the forefront: "Drifting Blues." "Drifting Blues" is the trio plus Johnny Otis on drums. It is that most basic of blues forms, the twelve-bar blues, a long way from anything Cole would have recorded. But Brown's vocal style is sophisticated and modern, as is the instrumental break by Moore and Otis.

The trio continued to be a popular act, although it was becoming more and more clear that the big draw was Brown, and in 1947 he left for a solo career to continued success. Arnold Shaw, in *Honkers and Shouters*, describes his style as "walk[ing] the line between urban blues and white torch songs," which is not a bad description of a mainstream jazz style. "Drifting Blues" has become a blues standard, with one interesting jazz treatment by Della Reese with Bill Doggett, Shelly Manne, Ray Brown,

Herb Ellis, and Bobby Bryant. Brown's career faltered during the 1950s but picked up again with a surprise hit in 1960, "Please Come Home for Christmas." He toured and recorded until his death in 1999, working with such jazz figures as Red Holloway, Houston Person, Roy Hargrove, and Marian McPartland. In 1973, he participated (on organ as well as piano) in a session led by T-Bone Walker and produced by Mike Stoller.[1]

Other than Charles Brown, the most direct connection to Cole was his protégé Nellie Lutcher, who was signed, on Cole's recommendation, to a recording contract with Capitol in 1947. Lutcher was born in Lake Charles, Louisiana, in 1912.

In general, the Black musicians who created the Los Angeles music scene of the 1940s could be divided into two groups—the Southern and Southwestern transplants, who played an instinctive music and brought soul to the Western capital, and the homegrown musicians, who had a background of formal training. Lutcher was the exception. The daughter of a bass player who led his own territory band, the Southern Rhythm

Figure 4.1. Nellie Lutcher, New York, between 1946 and 1948. William P. Gottlieb Collection, Library of Congress, Music Division.

Boys, she was raised on music . . . but not her father's music. Her mother took her to a local piano teacher, Mrs. Eugenia Reynaud, for instruction in the classics. Her mother, in fact, would not allow blues or jazz music in the house, but Nellie would sneak over to a friend's house to listen, particularly loving the playing of Earl "Fatha" Hines.

At twelve years old, according to local St. Charles historian Carolyn Woolsey, "She was playing 'The Blue Danube' for huge white-only black-tie audiences one night, and sitting in for Ma Rainey at Buster Mancuso's when the regular piano man went sick. Little Nellie had never played blues before, but she did fine."[2] At fourteen she was touring with her father's band, and at twenty-three, in 1935, she moved to Los Angeles to seriously focus on making a career as a musician. She paid her share of dues but began to be recognized, and in 1944 she made her first appearance on record, as part of Horace Henderson's orchestra backing up Lena Horne. Then on December 10, 1947, with her Capitol contract, she made her recording debut as featured performer, backed by a first rate jazz trio from Central Avenue, with Lee Young on drums, Ulysses Livingston on guitar, and Billy Hadnott on bass. Four songs were recorded, one of which, "Hurry on Down," became her first hit. For a second session, on April 20, Bob Crosby veteran Nappy Lamare replaced Livingston. The date yielded a second hit, "He's a Real Gone Guy," which rode the charts for twenty-three weeks. Lamare, although not as used to playing with her as Livingston, provides a nice counterpoint to her tricky and unique style of scat singing.

Those were Lutcher's biggest hits, but she continued to place records on the charts for the next three years, working with blue chip jazz musicians, including Irving Ashby and Big Sid Catlett. She recorded a range of material, much in the same way that Dinah Washington would. She took a very Cole-like approach to an Irving Berlin standard, "The Song Is Ended (But the Melody Lingers On)," and an insouciantly coquettish approach to a bluesy ballad, "Fine Brown Frame."

In 1950, Capitol paired her with Cole for two duets, with a band that included Ashby, Marshal Royal, and Charlie Barnet. The first was "For You My Love," written by pianist/bandleader/composer Paul Gayten, which had been a number one hit on the rhythm and blues charts for Larry Darnell the year before, and in which Lutcher brings out the blues side of Cole. The second, "Can I Come in for a Second?," is a mildly suggestive novelty dialog song by Sammy Cahn. Lutcher continued recording, always with first-rate jazz musicians, through the mid-1950s. After her recording career ended, she cut back on performing, appearing in a 1973 all-star show at Carnegie Hall headlined by Cab Calloway and featuring luminaries from Dizzy Gillespie to Louis Jordan. She died in 2007. Nina Simone has cited her as one of her greatest influences.

Another pianist-singer who was deeply influenced by Cole—he even recorded with Cole's guitarist Oscar Moore—was Ray Charles, who would go on to invent his own version of small-group swing which became so influential, original, and universally admired that he really falls outside of the scope of this book. But such was not always the case. In his 1965 book *Jazz Masters of the Fifties*, Joe Goldberg was one of the first to recognize Charles as one of those masters, devoting a chapter to him. In it, he recalls that when callers to Symphony Sid Torin's jazz radio show would request a Ray Charles number, they would be curtly told, "We don't play rock and roll."

Louis Jordan, to a remarkable extent, dominated the charts during the second half of the '40s, and his style was pretty close to inimitable. Perhaps the first artist to capture some of his insouciance and cleverness matched to a danceable beat would come in the next decade, in the person of Chuck Berry. But Jordan was not the only big band veteran to adapt his style to the new sound of small-group swing. Tiny Bradshaw began his career—primarily as a vocalist, although he played piano and drums—with Horace Henderson's Collegians in the 1920s. Moving to New York, he worked as a drummer and vocalist with various bands, including the Savoy Bearcats, before forming his own big band in 1934 and recording for Decca. In 1944, still with a big band (which included Sonny Stitt and "Big Nick" Nicholas), he cut two sides for Regis, a short-lived New York label that recorded some swing (Coleman Hawkins, Sid Catlett, the Cats and Fiddle) and some gospel. Then the band apparently toured, because later that same year they were captured on record while performing in Hollywood for Armed Forces Radio.

The lesson in the economics of touring with a big band must have sunk in to Bradshaw, because at the point where his recording career began in earnest, in 1947 with Savoy, he was down to five pieces with himself on vocals (plus two other names listed on the session log as "instrument unknown"). His Savoy outing, not hugely successful, could have felt very much at home in the mid-1930s, with the exception of the pared-back instrumentation: it was sugary ballads and bouncy mid-tempo numbers.

In 1949 Henry Glover, who had taken over the production reins at King Records, signed him. With Glover's input, he began moving in the direction of the contemporary sound in small-group swing, with more of the focus on a virtuoso soloist. Unfortunately, those first King recordings, like "Gravy Train," provide a tough lesson to Bradshaw. It's not true that any competent tenor sax player can pick up his instrument, blow a few honking notes, and become an instant Illinois Jacquet. Rufus Gore, a native Cincinnatian who was with King Records a long time and was a reliable section man, does not have the tone or the urgency, or really the musicality, to carry an extended solo. It was not until Red Prysock joined the ensemble in 1951 that the Bradshaw sound really coalesced. Listening to these Bradshaw tracks, in order, gives a mini-history of the development of soloist-oriented small-group swing in one band: small group recreating the big band sound ("These Things Are Love," Savoy); an early unsuccessful attempt to forefront a virtuoso soloist ("Gravy Train," King, Rufus Gore, tenor sax solo); finding the right soloist ("Bradshaw Boogie," King, Red Prysock, solo); and reaching the mature summit of the form ("Soft," King, Prysock).

Bradshaw was not the first to discover Wilburt "Red" Prysock's talent. From North Carolina, Prysock, like many of his generation, came of age in the army, where he learned to play the saxophone and fell under the influence of Lester Young. He headed for New York after his release and in 1947 joined up with guitarist Tiny Grimes. Grimes, who played a four-string tenor guitar, had impeccable jazz credentials. He had been a member of Art Tatum's trio and had recorded with Charlie Parker. He had also been a member of the swing quartet the Cats and the Fiddle, instrumentalist/singers known for showmanship as well as musicianship. Grimes formed his own band in 1944, a four-piece group that was a sort of harder-edged version of the sound of Johnny Moore's Three Blazers. His second group, the Tiny Grimes Swingtet, added Trummy Young on trombone and John Hardee on tenor sax. Its first session, for Blue Note, included a superfast version of "Flying Home," perhaps inspired by the lightning tempos of the beboppers.

Hardee was good and led his own "Swingtet" for Blue Note for a couple of years, but the band really came into its own with the addition of Prysock's powerful tenor sax in 1948. Grimes had recently signed with the newly formed Atlantic Records. Prysock was with Grimes for three years, with a side trip out to the West Coast, where he joined Roy Milton's Senders to make up an all-star saxophone lineup, with Jackie Kelso and Clifford Scott, who would strike glory a few years later playing the saxophone solo on Bill Doggett's "Honky Tonk." There's no super tenor sax battle here—as usual on Milton's records, the real star is Camille Howard—but some sensitive treatments of the blues. A more rousing tenor sax battle occurred on Grimes's recording of "Battle of the Mass," when a second tenor, Benny Golson, sat in. During this period, Grimes decided to call his group Tiny Grimes and his Rockin' Highlanders, which meant that, as a stage gimmick, they all appeared in kilts. That was the last straw for Red, and he quit.

Prysock signed with Mercury Records in 1954, and had his biggest hit record, "Hand Clappin'," in 1955. He would be with the label through the early '60s, although much of his work during those later years was unissued by the label. For one session, in 1958, he was given a big band with name jazz musicians like Taft Jordan and Emmett Berry, for a collection of standards. The album was titled *Swing Softly, Red*. The liner notes tried to place him within the "mainstream of jazz," despite his honkin' style:

Figure 4.2. Red Prysock, New York, between 1946 and 1948. William P. Gottlieb Collection, Library of Congress, Music Division.

Red Prysock is a tenor who swims smack dab in the mainstream of jazz. By mainstream I mean that belly part of jazz where many years ago you could find Coleman Hawkins, Chu Berry, Vido Musso, and literally hundreds of musicians who surrounded the melodic line with their big fat tones and pronounced vibrato and honked unashamedly with passion and muscle. The stamp of those swinging honkers is very evident on Red today, and if he has become a favorite of the rock 'n' roll crowd, it isn't because he especially asked for it. Actually, the only thing he has in common with various of the dignities of rock 'n' roll is the big beat. He is a far superior musician; his taste is a million light miles removed; and the beat is a coincidence—he got there first.

The album was released in 1961 and in spite of the apology—"He's not really rock and roll"—did not make much of a dent in the jazz market. Mercury had done well with jazz, but they misread the market here. Whereas a label like Prestige was successful marketing Willis "Gator Tail" Jackson to the soul jazz crowd, Mercury was trying to sell Prysock, who had never been known for big band swing, to an audience that mostly didn't exist. Further, they were doing a grave injustice to Prysock's contemporaries. Yes, he was an important musician who did not get the credit he deserved from a critical establishment that ghettoized his style of music. But he was far from the only one. With a performer like Red Prysock, as with so many who were making music in this era, the "now he's playing jazz, now he's selling out" distinction was an arbitrary one, made more by critics than by musicians. Were "Hand Clappin' " and "Soft" selling out because they were hit records? Was "Battle of the Mass" real jazz because Benny Golson was also on it? These people were musicians by trade—it was how they made their living—and musicians by passion, which they brought into the studio with them when they played music.[3] Atlantic Records, based in New York, quickly became the East Coast's leading label for small-group swing. Creating an East Coast version of the sound was not as easy as might have seemed, considering New York's reputation as a mecca for musicians. There were New York clubs that specialized in the traditional jazz style known as Dixieland, or sometimes "Chicago style" after Bix Beiderbecke, Frankie Trumbauer, and the group of young musicians who had come of age in that city. This style found its home at Nick's in Greenwich Village, and Jimmy Ryan's and Eddie Condon's on 52nd Street. It was a style of

Figure 4.3. Ahmet M. Ertegun and Nesuhi Ertegun, Washington, DC, ca. 1946–48. William P. Gottlieb Collection, Library of Congress, Music Division.

music that became increasingly the domain of white patrons. Meanwhile 52nd Street, for the most part, was becoming the in downtown spot for the new sound of bebop, the music that was being developed uptown in after-hours sessions at Minton's Playhouse and Monroe's Uptown House.

Ahmet Ertegun, who started Atlantic Records, was a musically savvy guy who had listened to Joe Liggins and Roy Milton, and knew that there was a new kind of music being made and an audience for it. Jerry Wexler, who shortly joined Atlantic, had even given it a name—as an editor at *Billboard*, he was responsible for changing the name of the Race Records chart to Rhythm and Blues. Ertegun and his brother Nesuhi were jazz lovers, attuned to the New York world of bebop, which was fast becoming the New York sound. In fact, in the early days when the new sound of modern jazz was developing, and a name for it had not yet been settled on, many people called it "New York music." Art Rupe, of Specialty Records, recalled in an interview with Arnold Shaw a comment that Ertegun made to him at the time: "Ahmet told me how lucky I had it because I went to New Orleans or produced out here [in LA], and I got musicians who did this thing naturally. But he had to take New York jazz people and make them try to copy our type of urban blues."

Wexler and the Erteguns put a lot of thought into the kind of sound they wanted. They first developed it for singer Ruth Brown, who would soon become so successful for them that Atlantic came to be known, following the popular nickname for Yankee Stadium, as "The House That Ruth Built." Brown, who was singing in a jazz club in Washington DC, was nonplussed when she heard that these white men wanted to sign her to the new blues label they were starting.

"Why me?" she asked. "I don't sing the blues. I hate the blues."

"Don't worry," they told her. "We're going be creating a whole new kind of blues."

Atlantic's initial output in 1947 was that of a new company finding itself. They issued some gospel. They tried out a couple of singers who didn't catch on. And they issued some jazz in various genres, including a couple of practitioners of small group swing. One was Tiny Grimes, who recorded for them once that year, and again in 1948 and 1949. The other was Joe Morris.

Morris, originally from Alabama, found his way to New York in the early 1940s, where he signed on with Lionel Hampton and made numerous recordings with him, including a couple of different versions of "Flying Home." Hampton used him as a writer/arranger as well as a trumpeter. When Morris left Hampton to form his own band, Atlantic was just getting started, and they would form a fruitful relationship. Wexler and the Erteguns understood the importance of a strong virtuoso soloist, particularly a tenor sax man, and so did Morris: his tenor player was Johnny Griffin, also a Hampton alumnus. They made their first recording session for the small independent Manor Records, which was short-lived but had a distinguished roster.

Morris and Griffin had learned well from their time with Hampton. Right out of the box they formed a tight band, capable of swinging and honking and making a record that was tight enough to work from beginning to end but loose enough to allow solos from both of them, plus—memorably on one of their Manor records, "Boogie Woogie Joe"—guitarist George Freeman. He hailed from a musical family; his brother and nephew were the saxophonists Von and Chico. The group came to Atlantic in December, 1947, for a December 10 session with a singer named Tony Mayo. Two songs were recorded that day, both little remembered, but they were back two days later, recording as Joe Morris and His Orchestra. It was an auspicious debut. They had a jukebox hit with "Low Groovin'," a midtempo blues featuring a Griffin solo, paired with "Jump with Me," where Griffin really has a chance to let loose and Freeman contributes a short, biting solo. This was New York music. It had that modern small-group swing sound, right for dancing, right for the jukeboxes and the rhythm and blues charts, played by musicians who had been to Minton's and to 52nd Street, and knew how to adapt the sounds of New York jazz to this increasingly popular genre. Griffin would go on to play with Art Blakey's Jazz Messengers, famously with Thelonious Monk, and as leader of his own groups. In 1948, Morris and Griffin were joined by Matthew Gee, Elmo Hope, Percy Heath, and Philly Joe Jones, and had a successful record in "The Applejack." This band stayed together through 1949.

In 1950, Morris had his first number one hit, "Anytime, Anyplace, Anywhere." Although the recording was credited to Joe Morris and His Orchestra with vocals by Laurie Tate, it was really Tate's record, and outside of Elmo Hope on piano and Roy Gaines on guitar, the musicians on the session are not credited. Morris moved to Herald Records in 1953 and had one last hit, accompanying Faye Adams, on his composition "Shake a Hand." The record went to number one and became a rhythm and blues standard.

Morris's success opened the door at Atlantic. In 1949, Frank "Floor-show" Culley, who had previously recorded as a member of Wynonie Harris's band, made his debut for the label, recording four songs. One of them was "Floor Show," from which he got his nickname. This was a not uncommon practice—giving a performer, particularly a bandleader, a nickname taken from his first big hit, but oddly enough, "Floor Show" was not Culley's big hit from that first session. That was "Cole Slaw," which went to number eleven on the Rhythm and Blues charts. It's unclear who made up the rest of his band, because by this time the record labels had come to accept the critical establishment's verdict that this music was not really jazz and so did not scrupulously make note of the sidemen on a session. It's believed that Randy Weston was on piano and Connie Kay on drums.

"Cole Slaw" was written by Jesse Stone, a veteran of the Kansas City scene who had come to New York in the 1930s and established himself as a writer/arranger for Chick Webb, Jimmie Lunceford, and other bands, white as well as Black—he arranged for Benny Goodman among others. His composition "Sorghum Switch" became a hit for Jimmy Dorsey in 1941, complete with a powerful solo for Dorsey. Rearranged for a contemporary Black small-group swing band, it became "Cole Slaw." Both versions have considerable virtues, and both have their place in the jazz canon. Stone was the only Black employee of Atlantic when it started, and he became their chief producer, the one most responsible for creating the Atlantic sound, that "new kind of blues" that Wexler and Ertegun promised Ruth Brown.

Frank Culley had a huge hit with "Cole Slaw," and a lesser but still noticeable hit with "Floor Show," and he kept recording for Atlantic. With Harry Van Walls on piano, he made his third hit record, Van Walls's bluesy piano and Culley's torchy saxophone taking "After Hour Session" to number ten on the *Billboard* chart. Van Walls, also known as Van "Piano Man" Walls, was much in demand as a player on jazz, small-group swing, rhythm and blues, and rock and roll sessions. Among his credits are Joe Turner's "Chains of Love," Ruth Brown's "5-10-15 Hours," the Clovers' "One Mint Julep," and Joe Morris's "Anytime, Anyplace, Anywhere." Culley remained active on Atlantic through 1951. On other labels, he recorded with Freddie Redd and Jimmy Rushing. In 1955, tunes of his were collected, along with some by Buddy Tate, for an LP given a title that awkwardly tried to appeal to two worlds: *Rock 'n' Roll Instrumentals for Dancing the Lindy Hop.*

Tab Smith, who had played with Basie, Jimmie Lunceford, and Coleman Hawkins, came to Atlantic in February 1949. Smith represented the romantic ballad side of small-group swing, a sound probably most associated with Earl Bostic. But it wasn't really the Atlantic sound, and Smith moved on to have one huge hit, the number one "Because of You," for United Records in 1951.

Ruth Brown made her first recording for Atlantic in April of 1949, with Amos Milburn on piano.[4] Next—perhaps Atlantic didn't quite know what do with her at first—she recorded "So Long," a beautiful ballad, and "Seems Like Old Times," a number associated with Guy Lombardo, with Eddie Condon's NBC Television Orchestra. By September, it seemed they were starting to figure out how to handle her. She recorded "I'll Get Along" with a band led by Budd Johnson, who had done well with his sister Ella Johnson and would work with her again, but her first number one hit, "Teardrops from My Eyes," featured Willis "Gator Tail" Jackson on tenor sax and Harry Van Walls on piano, both of whom would work with her many times. Brown credited Van Walls as being the musician most important in developing her sound, and Jackson was important to her in more ways: they lived together as husband and wife for several years.

Jackson got his start with Cootie Williams's band in 1949. Williams, best known for his work with Duke Ellington and Benny Goodman, had

Figure 4.4. Ruth Brown, 1955 publicity photo. Public domain.

formed his first band in 1941, around the same time as Lionel Hampton. Although he is not identified with one landmark recording as Hampton is with "Flying Home," he was equally important in pioneering, with a big band, the rhythm and blues sound that would develop as small-group swing. Over the years, he would employ Charlie Parker, Bud Powell, Eddie "Lockjaw" Davis, and Eddie "Cleanhead" Vinson, further blurring the line between contemporary jazz and rhythm and blues.

Jackson's first recording with Williams's band was "Gator Tail, Parts 1 and 2." He took the lead solo on the tune that gave him his nickname. "Gator Tail" moves from melodic, easy swing to ecstatic blowing, with a virtuoso display of honking. Until you hear it, it's hard to imagine how many different kinds of honks, squeals, and whistles can be put together, artfully and always musically, in one 78 RPM record. Williams and Jackson followed it up in their next session, later the same year, with "Doin' the Gator Tail," and he would keep the trademark alive in subsequent releases under his own name: "Later for the Gator," "Call of the Gator," "Gator's Groove," "Blue Gator," etc.

Jackson's first recording with his own group came in January 1950 for New York's Apollo label. The seven-piece band included Bill Doggett on piano and Panama Francis, who was ubiquitous on drums during the mid-twentieth century, playing traditional swing, the new small-group swing, rhythm and blues, rock and roll, modern jazz, soul, and even folk music. Jazzmen filled out the roster. It was a band that featured skilled, intuitive, and adaptable section men who knew how to swing. The Apollo session was a good showcase for Jackson's abilities as a player and band-leader: a tight arrangement that allowed for the ecstatic honking on "On My Own," backed with an old-school swing session on "Dance of the Lady Bug."

One more session for Apollo followed in May, and then Jackson started his run with Atlantic. In 1950, there was no particular reason to believe that Atlantic would outlast Apollo, let alone become the behemoth it turned into, but it proved to be the right move for Jackson on a personal as well as a career level: his first assignment was backing up Ruth Brown on "Teardrops from My Eyes." The label of the original release still credits "Ruth Brown with Budd Johnson's Orchestra," but the incomplete session notes list Willis Jackson on tenor sax and "probably Heywood Henry, baritone sax." The combination of Jesse Stone's production hand, two top saxophone players, and one of the finest singers in her genre all mesh on this recording. Henry's baritone rides under Brown's vocal, and Jackson's solo on the instrumental break adds without distracting.

Jackson next entered the Atlantic studios in July 1951 for an unchar-acteristic recording session: "Sentimental Rhapsody," drawn from the lush soundtrack music by film composer Alfred Newman for the 1931 movie *Street Scene*; a throwaway jump number called "Wine-o-Wine" featuring a quartet called the Four Gators; and the tune destined to become a moody cliché, "Harlem Nocturne," which had been written in 1939 for the Ray Noble orchestra. Jackson's version, oddly considering its title, was the first ever by a Black orchestra, and he does it nicely, but it's not exactly what one expects from the Gator. The "honkers," in general, prided themselves on their way with a ballad, but one expects a little honking on the session too. The musicians here are a new bunch, and on subsequent Atlantic recordings the personnel go unlisted. Jackson would rejoin Brown for her next number one hit, "5-10-15 Hours" and would continue to record with her, and on his own, through 1953.

Jackson next recorded for King Records. His first session there was Little Willie John's hit record, "All Around the World," on which he worked with pianist Champion Jack Dupree and guitarist Mickey Baker. He continued backing John and other King vocalists and made some records on his own. One of the last, in 1957, paired him with the great jazz guitarist Bill Jennings. It's not really inspired work by either of them, leaving behind the honking tenor small-group swing sound but not exactly arriving at anything else. But they kept working together, joined by organist Jack McDuff; by 1959 they had developed that new sound and were signed by Prestige Records, at that point one of the leaders of the new "soul jazz" movement, where they became, together and separately, among the most popular and most respected practitioners of this new sound.

CHAPTER FIVE

Open the Door

By the late 1940s, jazz with a beat was becoming one of the most commercially viable musical forms around. If it was still scorned by the jazz establishment, it was attracting some accomplished jazz musicians, who liked the idea of playing in a musical form that drew enthusiastic followers, who came to club dates and dances, and bought records. One of these was a veteran of the Los Angeles scene and the Lionel Hampton orchestra, tenor saxophonist Jack McVea.

McVea had one of the biggest and most surprising hits of 1947 with "Open the Door, Richard," an old vaudeville routine. It made McVea's name a household word, even to people who didn't know his tenor playing (which in fact is barely heard on the record). "Open the Door, Richard" was covered by numerous artists, including both Louis Jordan and Count Basie, not to mention Dusty Fletcher, the vaudeville comic who had made the routine famous on stage. "Richard" was McVea's only moment in a limelight of that magnitude, but he had a decent career, from big band to small-group swing, and finally to Disneyland.

McVea joined Lionel Hampton's band in 1941 on baritone sax and played baritone on the 1942 "Flying Home" session that launched Illinois Jacquet's career. He would join Jacquet in a tenor duet for one of the early Jazz at the Philharmonic concerts, playing the Count Basie/Lester Young tune "Lester Leaps In" with an all-star group. The nine-minute take, preserved on tape, was originally released on three sides of a 78 RPM album on Disc Records. *Norman Granz' Jazz at the Philharmonic Vol. 4.* Jacquet was by this time a star of JATP and was already developing the ecstatic honking, squealing style that would be the despair of jazz critics and the delight of audiences. McVea is a good match for him. But this is nine minutes of music, and includes solos by Nat "King" Cole and Les Paul, and it is a well-known swing classic, so the ecstatic tenor duel is worked up to gradually and becomes an integral part of a larger musical experience.

Ecstasy, though, is never simply an integral part. The Los Angeles audience, hip to this new sound of swing that was being invented in their hometown clubs, would have been waiting for it, and they were not to be disappointed. But still, it was only a part. A nine-minute performance is a lot of music, and it would incorporate a lot of the new ideas about music that McVea and others had been developing. For McVea, it had started when he left the swing band led by his father, who played "what was on paper. That's all. It was straight dance music." With the new groups he was joining, "We could play solos. I had never done that before." McVea joined a band led by Charlie Echols, featuring Herschel Evans and Don Byas (he had to take up the baritone to have a place in that lineup). He remembered, "That was the first time I saw wars, battles between the saxophonists. Byas and Evans, those guys were doing what the honkers were doing 15 years later." Improvisation and virtuoso solo playing were becoming as important to the musicians who would reinvent swing for the rhythm and blues era as they were to the musicians who would take apart the music and reconstruct it as bebop.

McVea formed his own band in 1945. They backed up Wynonie Harris and recorded some instrumental sides. He had performed "Open the Door, Richard" as early as 1944, on an Armed Forces Radio broadcast with a small group including Roy Eldridge and Barney Kessel, so it was no surprise when Slim Gaillard, in a 1945 recording, introduced him at the sound of knocking with "Open the door, Richard—it's Jack McVoutie and his tenor." Gaillard's number, a recreation of a casual jam session, became "Slim's Jam" and is probably better known to contemporary jazz audiences than "Open the Door, Richard," because of the other musicians that join Gaillard and "McVoutie" on the session: Dodo Marmarosa on piano, "Bam" Brown on bass, Zutty Singleton on drums, Dizzy Gillespie on trumpet, and, most significantly, "Charlie Yardbird-o-roonie." There's some patter, there's music, there are titans of bebop, swing, and rhythm and blues playing together, and enjoying it. It's all music. It's all jazz.

"Jack McVea and his All-Stars" were a shifting ensemble. At various times during the mid-1940s they included Marshal Royal, Russell Jacquet, Melba Liston, Irving Ashby, Jack Teagarden, and T-Bone Walker (McVea also played the tenor sax solo on Walker's "Call It Stormy Monday"). After his big hit, his group briefly became known as Jack McVea and His Door Openers, but it didn't stick.

McVea was born and bred a Los Angeleno, and remained based in the city throughout his career, although he did travel to Houston in 1950 to record with Clarence "Gatemouth" Brown, and to Florida in 1951 to record "St. Pete Florida Blues" with Ray Charles, a session that saw Charles breaking away from the Nat "King" Cole style and starting to add the gospel inflection to his blues singing that would soon see him changing American music irrevocably. During McVea's last phase, he led a Dixieland group at Disneyland.

Also hitting the top of the Race charts in 1947 was a two-sided hit for alto saxophonist/vocalist Eddie "Cleanhead" Vinson, with "Old Maid Boogie" (number one) and "Kidney Stew Blues" (number five). Vinson was one of those figures, like Illinois Jacquet, who was associated with rhythm and blues but also was accepted, provisionally, by the jazz community. Leonard Feather does include him in *The Encyclopedia of Jazz*, referring to the "coarse-toned but ruggedly swinging blues vein" in his alto sax playing and a vocal style that "has tended to become mannered but is still capable of authenticity."

From Texas, Vinson got his start with Milt Larkin's territory band, then toured with blues singer Big Bill Broonzy before joining Cootie Williams's big band in 1942. Williams, like Lionel Hampton, played big band swing with an edge that presaged the coming rhythm and blues revolution. And, like Hampton, his band was the starting point for a number of musicians who would go on to be part of the R&B and bebop revolutions, including Bud Powell, Eddie "Lockjaw" Davis, and Sam "the Man" Taylor. Vinson sang the blues with clear diction and slightly modernist phrasing in the style that became his trademark and that would later be made more famous by Joe Williams with Count Basie.

When Vinson left to form his own band in 1945, he started featuring himself much more on the alto sax, particularly on "Mr. Cleanhead Steps Out," a big band number reminiscent of "Flying Home." He signed with Mercury in 1946 and cut two sides in October with a big band, before coming back on November 18 with a smaller group to cut both "Old Maid Boogie" and "Kidney Stew Blues." "Old Maid Boogie" was the A side of Mercury's 78 RPM release and was the song that went to number one on the charts, but "Kidney Stew Blues" became a blues and swing standard, as well as his signature song. He would record it many more times: in New York in 1957 with his own band including Joe Newman and Paul Quinichette; in Chicago in 1961 with the Adderley Brothers and Joe Zawinul; in Paris in 1969 with Jay McShann, T-Bone Walker, and Hal Singer, to list a few.

Vinson would hit the charts again in 1949, with a band including Eddie "Lockjaw" Davis and Wynton Kelly, on "Somebody Done Stole My Cherry Red." His 1952 hit, "Person to Person," which went on to become a blues standard, featured Charlie Rouse, later to work for many others, but most significantly with Thelonious Monk. He would continue to tour, record, and play major blues and jazz festivals until his death in 1970.

By some reckoning the biggest rhythm and blues record of 1947—it is said, although this cannot be absolutely verified, to be the first million-seller in the genre—was Bull Moose Jackson's "I Love You, Yes I Do," an old-style ballad with a conventional pared-down big band arrangement, suggesting that the appetite for such music continued, nostalgic though it may have been by 1947.

Benjamin Joseph ("Bull Moose") Jackson had begun as a saxophone player with Lucky Millinder's orchestra but had been pressed into service as a vocalist on one night when Wynonie Harris could not make the gig and had discovered there was an audience for his voice. Syd Nathan's King Records, expanding from country and western to Race music, had tried to sign Millinder, but he was signed to Decca, and he recommended Jackson, who stayed with Nathan and began a successful career, first on Queen, which Nathan had thought to set up as his Race Records subsidiary, then with King as Nathan quickly decided one label was enough.

Jackson's first session for Queen/King, in August 1945, was blues-oriented and included a cover of "Honeydripper," a swing band arrangement that was virtually a solid instrumental, with one short vocal chorus near the end to remind listeners what they were hearing. Jackson had put together an excellent swing band primarily of Millinder and Cootie Williams veterans, with Sam "the Man" Taylor pairing with him on tenor sax, Sir Charles Thompson on piano, and Panama Francis on drums. Other band members—trumpeter Harold "Money" Johnson, alto saxophonist Burnie Peacock, guitarist Bernie MacKay, and bassist Beverly Peer—had solid resumes in the era's jazz bands and would continue to have long careers as sidemen.

This was one of the finest small-group swing ensembles of the mid-1940s, with a front line of musicians who knew how to play in an ensemble and could swing out in their solos. They backed up vocalist Anisteen Allen in December 1945. Allen was a fine vocalist, and Jackson's group brought out the best in her and made this a session (they recorded nine songs) to remember. Also in December, swelled out to big band size and billed as Panama Francis and His Miamians, and then as the Bull Moose Jackson/Panama Francis Orchestra, they cut several sides, some of them with vocalist Leo Ketchum, who worked with Millinder and Jackson for a couple of years, but seems not to have much of a career beyond that. There were no vocals by Jackson during this period.

On a few sessions with Millinder in 1946, he took some vocals—as did several other singers—but not until the "I Love You, Yes I Do" session did he really step out as a vocalist. This was a turning point in his career. From 1947 on, he was primarily and then exclusively a vocalist. He would never again work with a band quite as good as that first band, although they were always good. Frank Wess was in his band for a while, as were Benny Golson, Bill Doggett, and Red Prysock.

Jackson's other significant turning point came in 1952, when he recorded an off-color blues, "Big Ten-Inch Record." It was clever and funny as well as danceable, and more than a little off-color. If it wasn't

Figure 5.1. King Records' label for "Big Ten-Inch Record," 1952. Public domain.

exactly a hit (it was too dirty for radio), it became a sort of underground hit and became his trademark song, always requested at his live shows. And it became the vehicle for a comeback of sorts. In 1981, two decades after his career had wound down and he was working catering jobs in Washington, DC, an area disc jockey who knew him heard a popular local band performing "Big Ten-Inch Record" and told the group that he could get Bull Moose Jackson to come and perform it with them. They were thrilled, and he had a mini-revival.

Vocalists had been part of the supporting cast for much of the swing era, a situation that changed dramatically in the new decade for a variety of reasons: the extraordinary popularity of Frank Sinatra, the two-year virtual disappearance of instrumental musicians during the Petrillo strike, changing economics, and changing tastes. So instrumental small-group swing came along at a time when instrumental popular music had become a niche, a small part of the tableau of rhythm and blues. Nat "King" Cole had been a touchstone in many ways for this transition, but one wouldn't expect him to come up in a discussion of Bull Moose Jackson; yet once again, he's relevant. Cole's success as a vocalist came to overshadow his prowess as a jazz pianist, to the extent that most people only think of him as a vocalist and may not be aware that he played the piano at all. Jackson's career was modest compared to Cole's, but most of those rhythm and blues aficionados who collect his records and discuss him on R&B fan sites may never have even heard his instrumental tracks; yet they represent his best work and some of the finest small-group swing.

As popular as the vocalists were becoming, there was still room for swinging instrumental releases with a strong hook and a back beat—tunes that could galvanize an instant response on a two-and-a-half-minute record but could be opened for an extended outing on the dance floor. Catching that elusive hitmaking quality was like catching lightning in a bottle, but some musicians made it. One such was saxophonist Hal Singer.

Singer was an infant when his family's home was burned to the ground in the Tulsa race massacre of 1921. They escaped and moved to Kansas City, where he grew up in one of the most fertile musical environments of the day. His parents wanted him to study the violin, but Lester Young was in Kansas City, and his example was too tempting to resist. By 1943, Singer had joined the hottest band in Kansas City, Jay McShann's, the band with which, a year earlier, Charlie Parker had recorded "Sepian Bounce." Moving on to New York, he worked with Roy Eldridge and recorded a session with Don Byas, backing up a vocalist. But the new sound was beckoning to him, and in 1947, he joined Tiny Bradshaw to record a session with Big Maybelle for King Records. Oran "Hot Lips" Page was with Bradshaw then, and Singer left to join Page, recording with Lonnie Johnson, Marion Abernethy, Big Maybelle, and Wynonie Harris. In 1948, he formed his own band and signed with Savoy Records.

Singer had a good band and a good idea of what he wanted to do. On trombone, he had the veteran Milt Larkin, whose Southwestern territory band had launched the careers of Illinois Jacquet, Arnett Cobb, Eddie "Cleanhead" Vinson, and so many others. His piano player was sixteen-year-old Wynton Kelly. Bassist Franklin Skeete, also at the beginning of his career, would go on to play with many of the top rhythm and blues acts, and then with Lester Young, Bud Powell, Max Roach, and other top names in the bebop field. Heyward Jackson came to Singer from Mercer Ellington's band.

Singer hit pay dirt on his very first recording session. "Corn Bread" was built on a blues riff, in fact a few blues riffs pulled from here and there, with a growling low note from the trombone and the lower register of the tenor saxophone, keeping the rhythm solid, throwing in a few melodic surprises to put a little kick under the dancers, building to a honking crescendo. *Billboard* hailed it as "surefire race-box material with its obvious emphasis on rhythm and raucous tenor and bary sax blowing!"—although it was Larkin's trombone, not a baritone sax.

"Corn Bread" went to number one and made Singer pretty much of a one-hit wonder. Along with its follow up, "Beef Stew," it kept him working, although it was something of a mixed blessing. Right after making the record, he had landed his dream job, playing with Duke Ellington's orchestra. But everywhere they played, audiences kept calling for "Corn Bread." He had to make a choice, and it was an economic as well as an artistic dilemma: remain a part of the world's most prestigious jazz orchestra, at a section man's wages, or take the money that was being offered to him as a headliner with a hit record? He chose the latter, and that became his career. With the ability to lay down a good groove and improvise over it, plus the ability to attract the finest musicians (Billy Taylor, Grachan Moncur, Tyree Glenn, Gene Ramey, Milt Hinton, Sam "the Man" Taylor, and Mickey Baker were just a few), he recorded for Mercury, Savoy, Atlantic, DeLuxe, and King all through the 1950s, toured with Charles Brown, the Orioles, and other rhythm and blues acts, and began playing regularly at the Metropole, New York's traditional jazz club, with Roy Eldridge, Coleman Hawkins, and others. When soul jazz became the new thing in the 1960s, he recorded with leading jazz independent Prestige Records. Later, after a European tour with Earl Hines, he settled in France and had a whole new career there.

One of the biggest hits of the year—and one that went on to have a continuing impact—was unusual in that it came from an alto saxophonist. And even more unusual, it boasted an even more influential alto saxophonist among its musical godfathers. The hit's creator was Paul Williams, who was born in Lewisburg, Tennessee, in 1915, grew up in Bowling Green, Kentucky, and moved to Detroit when he was thirteen. It was in that city, which came to be known as a breeding ground for jazz musicians in the mid-twentieth century, that he took up music; by the time World War II came around he was already leading his own dance band there. The war broke up his band, and he played with various groups. All of his bookings in those days were for white-only dances, and he played the popular tunes of the day, with arrangements that were used by the white bands of the day. It was not until 1945, when he joined a band led by Clarence Dorsey, that he played for his first Black audience.

Later that year, Williams hooked up with another Detroiter, James Pope, better known by his stage name of King Porter, and he began to develop a distinctive style. It was the era when saxophonists were finding that swagger and showmanship that would set them apart and make them stars. Williams played alto and baritone, rather than tenor, but he had the style, plus the tone, to carry it off. Savoy Records, which was recording many of the top modern jazz names and had hit the rhythm and blues market with Hal Singer, signed him up at the urging of producer Teddy Reig, who had been producing jazz records for them.

Williams's early career with Savoy is interesting for a couple of different reasons. All his early recordings, and almost all of his records for Savoy, were made in Detroit, and largely with unheralded musicians who stayed close to home, and have little or no discography beyond their work with Williams and Porter. But there were a lot of very good musicians in Detroit, and Williams's work holds up in comparison with bands that employed musicians with more distinguished pedigrees. Second, more than most in the rhythm and blues field, Williams stuck to instrumental small-group swing. He used vocalists seldom, and they tended to be undistinguished. Third, Williams's output is remarkable for its sheer volume. His first session for Savoy was on September 5, 1947. He cut four songs, one of which, "Hastings Street Bounce," sold modestly well, mostly in the Detroit area. Then after that his recording dates are October 6, 1947 (four tunes), November 20 and 21, 1947 (six tunes), December 1947 (no date specified, four tunes), December 18, 1947 (eight tunes), December 23, 1947 (four tunes), and December 30, 1947 (eight tunes). His schedule in 1948 was much the same. A couple of these sessions were booked under King Porter's name and a couple under Wild Bill Moore. A couple were recorded in LA for Imperial, but most were in Detroit for Savoy, and Savoy released almost all of them.

The economics of this, for Savoy, were fairly simple. Herman Lubinsky, the label's owner, was notoriously cheap, and he was no doubt relying on the enthusiasm of the young Detroiters, who were probably lucky to make back their carfare to the studio. And he was having some success. "Bouncing with Benson," from the October session, sold some copies, and "35-30" was a regional hit. Williams was developing a following.

Wild Bill Moore was a Detroiter who had left home to achieve a considerable measure of success, mostly in Los Angeles. He had played on a number of radio broadcasts with Louis Armstrong during the Petrillo strike. He had worked with Slim Gaillard, Jack McVea, Big Joe Turner, and Dexter Gordon. As a member of Bill Doggett's band, he had played the tenor sax solo on Helen Humes's hit record, "Be-Baba-Leba." Returning to Detroit in 1947, he would score a hit record, "We're Gonna Rock," with Savoy, and work extensively with Williams and Porter, later seeing a career revival in soul jazz.

Also joining Williams in 1948 was trumpeter Phil Guilbeau, who had one of those "musician's musician" careers: always in demand but gaining little name recognition. One of his steadier gigs was with Count Basie, and perhaps his moment in the sun came when Ray Charles requested him and had him flown in to play on his *Genius + Soul = Jazz* album. Guilbeau arrived with no idea of what was expected of him, and Quincy Jones, producing the session, had no idea what to tell him. Clark Terry, sitting next to him in the trumpet section, had to nudge him to let him know when to come in. Later, he discovered that Charles, who left nothing to chance, had planned it this way. He knew exactly what Guilbeau could do and wanted the spontaneity he would get from bringing him in unrehearsed.

Guilbeau was with Williams, although Moore was not, on December 18, 1948, when they went into the studio to record four tunes. Williams had only recently, on the strength of "35-30," begun touring outside Detroit; one of his early gigs was in Baltimore, where he shared a bill with Lucky Millinder and heard Millinder rehearsing a tune by his trumpet player,

Andy Gibson, which Williams liked. The name of the tune was "D'Natural Blues," and when Williams brought it in to his December 18 session, his producer, Teddy Reig, liked it, too. He had liked it once before, when Charlie Parker brought it to *his* first recording session, also produced by Reig for Savoy. Then it had been called "Now's the Time." "It's not the same tune," Williams said later in an interview, and perhaps it's not, but it certainly has the same opening riff. Williams changed the name of the tune to something more contemporary sounding. Just as Joe Liggins had written "The Honeydripper" to fit a popular current dance, the Texas Hop, so Williams arranged this tune to fit a currently popular dance and named it after the dance: "The Hucklebuck."

Savoy's Herman Lubinsky hoped he might have another hit like "Cornbread," but "The Hucklebuck" exceeded his wildest dreams. It spent thirty-two weeks on the Race Records charts and was covered by everyone, Black or white: Lionel Hampton had a version and Roy Milton, as did Tommy Dorsey and Frank Sinatra. It crossed cultural boundaries when Italian-American singer Lou Monte recorded it as a sort of tarantella, with lyrics in a rapid-fire Italian doubletalk. Chubby Checker would later record it as a twist.

Much is made of the proposition that bebop was created as a music you couldn't dance to. That was kind of true in New York, where a sur- tax on clubs that allowed dancing made the owners of small jazz clubs discourage it. But outside of New York, you could dance to "Now's the Time," and people did, although the tempo was a lot faster, and if Charlie Parker was playing, you might want to just stop and listen to improvisations of genius. Paul Williams on baritone sax and Phil Guilbeau on trumpet both take tasty solos on "The Hucklebuck," but it's for dancing all the way through. Andy Gibson received composer credit for "The Hucklebuck"; none went to Charlie Parker. It probably didn't matter. Herman Lubinsky was well known for sewing up the publishing rights to anything recorded in his studio, so he would have been the only one to make any serious money on it.

If anyone was going to make a successful career in the new genre of jazz with a beat, it was Cecil McNeely, who had bought classical recordings, studied music in school, played with the most progressive of West Coast beboppers, studied more with a classical teacher from one of Los Angeles's premier symphony orchestras—and then figured out how to find the most popular new sound of his day and take it to its most extreme manifestation.

He grew up listening to classical music and said that he shopped at "record stores [which] were mainly for white people. They had classical music . . . Ravel, Bach, Beethoven. I remember my favorites: Debussy, Stravinsky and I liked Richard Strauss very much . . . 'Death and Transfiguration.' " He also

> studied composition with Lloyd Reese. Lloyd Reese taught Eric Dolphy; Harry Carney also studied with him and so did Ben Webster and Buddy Collette, to name a few. Art Tatum highly recommended him. When Art found out I was studying with Lloyd, he asked me to come and play for him.
>
> So I'm saying briefly that people don't know what a black man . . . what it took to make a jazz musician. In my young days, we were raised more on classical music than on any other kind. It was the only music we were exposed to, other than the church choir. I wasn't raised in a night club. I wasn't raised in a whore house (there wasn't any music in them, anyway).

He played modern jazz with Sonny Criss and Hampton Hawes, and studied theory and harmony with Joseph Cadaly of the RKO Symphony Orchestra.

And then he learned to forget all that and listen to what the audience wanted to hear—a sound that started with Illinois Jacquet and took off from there. That was what he was playing when Ralph Bass, a producer and talent scout for Savoy, heard him playing on Central Avenue and signed him to Savoy Records, where label owner Herman Lubinsky immediately recognized these sounds were not coming from a man named Cecil and changed his name to Big Jay. Bass tabbed him as a good prospect to be the next Hal Singer or Wild Bill Moore.

McNeely was ready. He was realizing that he would never do what Criss and Hawes were beginning to do. He didn't have the temperament, perhaps he didn't have the vision. And he was beginning to wonder if all the serious studying he was doing might have its own limitations: "Counterpoint, vocal harmony, classical conservatory, clarinet too . . . I got real legit, my saxophone began to sound like a cello and it seemed like my soul had just left momentarily 'cause of studying so hard. I was obsessed with notes. So when Ralph Bass signed me up with Savoy, I had to let myself go."

McNeely is a curious and interesting study. When people talk about the excesses of the rhythm and blues saxophone—the honking, the screeching, the theatrics, walking the bar, playing on their backs—they're generally thinking of Big Jay, who did have a tendency to sacrifice musicality for theatricality. Yet his first record for Savoy—oddly, because Ralph Bass had specifically signed him for his theatricality, to be the wild man of the tenor sax—was the mellow, Erskine Hawkins–like "Benson's Groove," recorded on October 9, 1948. But "Benson's Groove," titled at Lubinsky's suggestion as a tribute to popular Chicago disc jockey Al Benson, won McNeely some notice when it became Benson's theme song. It was followed just two weeks later with a second session, which was to produce McNeely's first hit.

McNeely has said that he got the inspiration for "The Deacon's Hop" from a Glenn Miller record: "I was a regular visitor to Pete Canard's record shop at 98th and Compton Ave . . . Pete played me Glenn Miller's 'Nothing But Soul,' and that was it. That drum sound, tch tut tut tch, just a sock cymbal. From that I wrote the tune, just from that little introduction." "Deacon's Hop" is a long way from Glenn Miller, but it's also a short way from being a finished composition. Adapting Lester Young's solo from Count Basie's 1940 recording of "Broadway," McNeely shows that he can play and that he can generate excitement on record, but his hard-driving effects are obtained at some cost to unity. Still, it served notice that a formidable new talent had arrived—one who was not afraid to pull out all the stops, a promise he made good in his live performances, which became ever more popular.

McNeely preferred to limit those live performances to his native California, which did not sit well with Lubinsky, so he soon cut off his association with Savoy and recorded for West Coast labels, Exclusive and Imperial. He would also record, over the next couple of decades, with Aladdin, Federal, Vee-Jay, and Swingin'. McNeely would continue to live up to his reputation as the wild man of the tenor sax, but he was more than that, making records that impress to this day with their virtuosic intensity. And in 1959, he had a surprise hit record with a ballad, "There Is Something on Your Mind," with a vocal by Little Sonny Warner and a sensitive saxophone solo.

On a comeback concert in 1989, he was playing on November 9 at the Quasimodo Club in West Berlin, near the Berlin Wall. As was his habit, he led his band and his audience out into the street, and some say he blew so hard that the wall came tumbling down. Well, as The Man Who Shot Liberty Valance once said, "print the legend." And the wall did come down that night.

McNeely had a long and successful career. He broke boundaries. He made music. And his horn was featured on a cover of Smithsonian Magazine. And his power to move audiences was well summarized by a review in one of Los Angeles's Black newspapers, *The Sentinel*, of his appearance at the 5th Annual Cavalcade of Jazz, held in LA's Wrigley Field in 1949 and featuring Lionel Hampton as the nominal headliner:

> Hamp presented his latest and brightest stars to the afternoon's program, but it was local sax-tooter Jay McNeely who dipped his golden tenor in rhythm and walked away with all the honors!
>
> Some of our younger fry hopped on the McNeely bandwagon when the big smilin' tenor-tooter first appeared on the music scene at the Barrel House nearly a year ago. Your reviewer must admit this is the first time I have ever paid scant attention to Big Jay . . . [but] we honestly believe he'll make musical history before this year rolls into oblivion . . .
>
> Big Jay and his boys . . . blew some of the weirdest, wildest, rockingest and swingingest music heard around this neck of the woods since the Basie band first popped in port many years ago.
>
> This guy McNeely is a showman. He went through the stands blowing his horn. He walked around the field sweating, swearing and swinging! It was a hot day at Wrigley Field, but Big Jay blew. It was a pleasure to watch him. Watta horn-tooter!

If one couldn't get wilder than McNeely, another jazzman—like others who found success on the rhythm and blues charts, a Lionel Hampton alumnus—found as different a path to success as it is possible to get. Earl Bostic is probably best known for his smooth rhythm and blues hits: "Temptation" in 1948, "Flamingo" in 1951, and "Harlem Nocturne" in 1956. Among jazz fans, he may also be known for his work with territory bands, including Bennie Moten, or for his recordings with Lionel Hampton and "Hot Lips" Page, or perhaps for the future jazz stars (including John Coltrane) that he mentored in his bands. And perhaps even for his work as an arranger, for Paul Whiteman, Louis Prima, Lionel Hampton, Jack Teagarden, Artie Shaw, and others.

Among jazz musicians, he was widely considered to be, technically, the greatest alto saxophonist who ever lived, which is an extreme statement, but those who spent time around him, who heard him play at

Minton's Playhouse, will swear by it. Lou Donaldson recalled, "The man could play three octaves. I mean play 'em, I don't mean just hit the notes. He was bad. He was a technician you wouldn't believe." John Coltrane joined Earl Bostic's band because of what he could learn: "He showed me a lot of things on my horn. He has fabulous technical facilities and knows many a trick." And Benny Golson recalls going to Minton's with Coltrane in 1950 to hear Bostic, and sitting and talking with him afterward: "We heard Bostic play in any key, any tempo, playing almost an octave above the range of the alto saxophone. We talked with him and he told us how each brand of saxophone should sound. He said, 'On the Martin you finger it this way, the Buescher is that way, and like so on the Selmer.'" Art Blakey agreed: "If Coltrane played with Bostic, I know he learned a lot. Nobody knew more about the saxophone than Bostic. I mean technically, and that includes Bird. Bostic could take any make of saxophone and tell you its faults and its best points. Working with Earl Bostic is like attending a university of the saxophone."

Even understanding that Bostic's records only hint at his abilities, they still show a lot. "Flamingo" may only begin to suggest his range, but his emotional expressiveness comes through. With Jimmy Cobb on drums, it also surprises with its improvisational ingenuity, a quality not always prized in rhythm and blues instrumentals, which are based in the swing traditions. "Up There in Orbit," from 1958, shows more of his technical virtuosity, as he plays several bars considerably above the range that an alto saxophone is supposed to be able to reach, with every note clear. Bostic always played tunes with a strong melody and always had his drummer keep that steady back beat, so his jukebox dance audience was never in danger of getting lost. Drummer Roy Porter, who played with Bostic (also with Howard McGhee, Charles Mingus, Dizzy Gillespie, and Charlie Parker) recalls how Bostic, also a master drummer, taught him the "double shuffle with a back-beat": "I'd been doing a single shuffle with the right hand on the cymbal, while the left hand was doing a back-beat on two and four. The double is with both hands shuffling, keeping the back-beat going too. No easy task at some tempos, but it makes for a heavier beat. He was an amazing musician."

A lot is written about jazz musicians "slumming," playing beneath themselves, abasing themselves for the money by playing rhythm and blues. Sonny Criss, whose gifts were never fully recognized, and who ultimately committed suicide in 1974, said just that of his old friend, Big Jay McNeely: "[He] could play for a while. Something happened. Money got to him." John Coltrane is often used as an example. And it's true—playing rhythm and blues was not what Coltrane wanted to do with his career, his talent, or his unique vision. But Coltrane wouldn't have been happy or fulfilled playing with Benny Goodman either, and that doesn't make Goodman's music inferior or "not real jazz."

Cecil McNeely, with his classical training, his years of study, his early experience playing with Sonny Criss and Hampton Hawes, could have made career choices other than becoming Big Jay McNeely. Earl Bostic, with his formidable chops, his encyclopedic knowledge of instruments, and the sounds that could be gotten from them, could have brought those gifts to bear on records other than "Temptation," "Flamingo," and "Harlem Nocturne." So why didn't they play real jazz?

Art and art forms are defined in different ways at different times, and back in the 1940s and '50s much was made of what was "real jazz" and what wasn't. The definitions could become so narrow that even Louis Armstrong could find himself left out in the cold, as he was by the *DownBeat* reviewer who gave short shrift to his performance in the movie *High Society* and dismissed his performance of "Now You Has Jazz" with Bing Crosby: "Jazz? I'm still waiting to hear it." The musicians playing swing recalibrated for a new decade, which was marketed as "rhythm and blues," tended to accept this exclusion, as though the inclusion of either rhythm or blues in one's music should somehow disqualify one as a jazz musician. Big Jay McNeely, who told *Jazzwax*'s Marc Myers that he considered himself "a jazz musician who played for people who wanted to dance," at the same time mostly accepted the definitions that excluded him, telling Myers in the same interview:

> I didn't play with a real legit jazz sound. For that sound you'd use very little lip, what they called a nonpressure embouchure . . . Just enough pressure on the reed to make it vibrate. I took the same principles I learned in vocal lessons and applied it for a good, big soulful sound on the saxophone . . . I started out playing jazz but I didn't have a perfect ear, like Sonny Criss did. Guys like Sonny could pick up their horn and play anything. They heard things once and they could go off on it.

So McNeely accepted the role that had been assigned to him as being outside the circle of real jazz, but at the same time it chafed at him. When Myers asked him, "Did jazz artists dig you?" he replied: "Hamp

[Hawes], Bird, Miles, Sonny [Criss]—they all loved what I did. Dizzy, too. I played Birdland in New York in the early 1950s and opened for jazz artists. They'd put me on first, before Milt Jackson, Ben Webster, Erroll Garner, all of them. I was always the opener. I guess to get the people who were there excited."

It's hard to say why Earl Bostic made the choices he did. Jazz artists recognized his unique ability. Lou Donaldson recalled: "Bostic was down at Minton's and Charlie Parker came in there. They played 'Sweet Georgia Brown' or something and he gave Charlie Parker a saxophone lesson." But at the same time Donaldson faulted him for "play[ing] stuff that I'd consider corny." He once asked Bostic why he didn't utilize all of his formidable technique on his records, and Bostic replied, "Don't play anything you can play good on a record. People will copy it." This was an attitude not uncommon in the teens and '20s, when recording was still new, but unusual in the '50s. And given Bostic's technical ability, it's hard to imagine very many people being able to duplicate his sound, even after hearing it on a record. Drummer Earl Palmer, who played several gigs with Bostic, considered him the equal of Charlie Parker technically but said he "wasn't as hip." And perhaps he wasn't, but then again who was?

Other musicians who played the music that was marketed as rhythm and blues were less inclined to simply accept that their music was something other than and aesthetically inferior to jazz. These included Bill Doggett and Sil Austin, both of whom had hit instrumentals in the rock and roll era ("Honky Tonk" and "Slow Walk"; see chapter 7). Austin, chafing against the consensus to pigeonhole him, said: "Now, it's hard to think of my 'Slow Walk' without thinking about Bill Doggett's 'Honky Tonk,' and I've talked to Bill about this. Our records got called rock 'n' roll. Now, we'd always played like the way we did. I was hanging out with Sonny Rollins and Jackie McLean. All we were doing was playing great horn."

CHAPTER SIX

Down in New Orleans

New Orleans would rise and fall several times as a music center during the twentieth century. Music historians argue the question of whether the Crescent City was really the birthplace of jazz, but none can deny its importance in the germination and growth of America's music, with figures like Buddy Bolden, Jelly Roll Morton, Sidney Bechet, King Oliver, and Louis Armstrong. It's argued that these seminal figures brought jazz to the rest of America, but they did so (with the exception of Bolden, who died before he could ever be recorded) by leaving New Orleans and working in Chicago, New York, Los Angeles, and Europe.

Plenty of musicians stayed behind, but the scene and the importance of the city as a center for new music went into a decline. The "moldy figs" like Heywood Hale Broun and Steven Smith revived interest in the "real jazz" of New Orleans in 1939–40, but they were early archivists. Broun did record Kid Rena leading a group of the old-time musicians, but this was for a small group of enthusiasts, primarily in New York and San Francisco, and in no way could it have been considered the start of a new recording boom.

But in the postwar years, the new Black popular music—small-group swing, rhythm and blues—that was exciting a new generation of musicians in Los Angeles and New York, Chicago and Detroit, was having the same effect on the musicians of New Orleans. Music was being made in New Orleans, and it was happening despite the lack of any music business in the city. The record labels like Specialty or Imperial that heard about the new breed of New Orleans musicians, and signed them to recording contracts, were on the West Coast. An even earlier label to discover this music was an East Coast label out of New Jersey, DeLuxe Records. It was founded in 1944 by two sons of Hungarian Jewish immigrants, David and Jules Braun, with an eye on the emerging Black market for new music. In 1947, they heard about what was happening in New Orleans and went down to check it out. Their first two signings were Paul Gayten and Dave Bartholomew.

Gayten was a Louisiana native, born in 1920 in Kentwood, near the Mississippi border. As a teenager, he played piano and toured with a couple of show bands, where he had to learn to read music and play anything in the band's repertoire, which was varied and extensive. After that, he led his own band, which featured future jazz saxophone star Teddy Edwards. Gayten was drafted into the army during World War II. He didn't exactly see the world with the army, being stationed in Biloxi, Mississippi, but he did continue to develop musically, leading the base's army band. After the war, he headed for New Orleans. An avid student with a deep love of music, he was a fluent reader and could play blues or bebop, barrelhouse or Beethoven.

When DeLuxe signed him, Gayten was one of New Orleans's most popular bandleaders. He also did a lot of work with a trio, which meant, as with every piano trio of his day, that he felt the influence of Nat "King" Cole, but even more of Charles Brown. Closer to home, right in Kenwood, he had the influence of his uncle, blues great Little Brother Montgomery. But New Orleans was an insular world, with its own traditions, and piano players there cast a long shadow, starting with Jelly Roll Morton and including Tuts Washington, who played a unique New Orleans blend of ragtime, boogie-woogie, and blues.

Gayten's first session with DeLuxe saw him backing up blues singer Cousin Joe, with a five-piece band. Cousin Joe's career never took off, but the session was noteworthy as the debut of three figures who were to make a significant mark in New Orleans music: Gayten, tenor saxophonist Lee Allen, and sound engineer Cosimo Matassa, who had dropped out of Tulane University (he'd been a chemistry major) to open a recording studio in back of his parents' shop on Rampart Street.

Gayten soon had his first top ten hit on the Race charts, coming from one of his first recording sessions, accompanying vocalist Annie Laurie on "Since I Fell for You." At almost the same time, he landed another record on the charts: "True," performed in more of a Nat "King" Cole Trio or Three Blazers style and featuring his own vocals. But a solo career was not in his future. Gayten would have a few more hits with

Annie Laurie and go on to become a very successful behind-the-scenes figure, as bandleader, songwriter, producer, and record company executive, particularly working with Chicago's Chess Records. There he did a bit of everything, from producing to promoting to talent scouting to leading a band, eventually becoming the head of operations for Chess on the West Coast, where he was one of the first Black record company executives in Los Angeles and had a house across the street from Nat "King" Cole.

Gayten made a few records for Chess subsidiaries Checker and Argo. The best of these are "The Music Goes Round and Round," a popular jazz standard from the 1920s, which features Gayten's vocal and an uncredited but very good tenor saxophonist; and "Nervous Boogie," with some first rate boogie-woogie piano playing against an ensemble backing. Boogie-woogie was not exactly cutting edge music in 1958, although archivist and ragtime pianist Johnny Maddox had scored a surprise megahit a couple of years earlier with his "Crazy Otto Medley." Nonetheless, hit material or no, it gave Gayten a showcase for his considerable talents at the keyboard.

New Orleans, as a musical center, was different. The other musicians we've discussed got their start in the swing bands of Chick Webb, Lionel Hampton, Cootie Williams, or Les Hite. Or they played in the South-western territory bands that got their direction from Kansas City and the muscular progressive swing of Bennie Moten and Count Basie. Dave Bartholomew, on the other hand, while he did play briefly with Jimmie Lunceford, cut his musical teeth in the 1930s with Oscar "Papa" Celestin and with Mississippi riverboat show bands. Celestin had nurtured the careers of King Oliver and Louis Armstrong, but after the jazz world's attention turned away from New Orleans, he had become a popular French Quarter tourist attraction, playing "Muskrat Ramble" and "Royal Garden Blues" for the Bourbon Street and Jackson Square crowd. The riverboat show bands were similarly not aimed at jazz cognoscenti, but for tourists out for a good time and a trip back into history.

One might think that this would have put New Orleans musicians at a disadvantage in the competition to create new sounds for the post-war era, but such was not the case. In the first place, there's no simple linear progression in the development of jazz. Avant garde musicians of the 1960s did not necessarily check off the bebop and hard bop boxes on their way to a new sound. Ornette Coleman had played rhythm and blues; Steve Lacy went straight from Dixieland to the avant garde; Garvin Bushell's experience ran the gamut from Bunk Johnson to John Coltrane. In the second place, New Orleans may have dropped off the radar screen of the jazz establishment, to the point where even Louis Armstrong had become an also-ran in jazz polls, but it was still an intensely musical city. It had musicians like Papa Celestin, Kid Rena, and Louis "Big Eye" Nelson, who were still playing. It had the riverboat, street, and marching bands, as well as bands that played on the backs of flatbed trucks. Bartholomew's first introduction to music, he would tell an interviewer, came from following those flatbed trucks when they drove through his neighborhood. Music in New Orleans ran rich and deep. So when rhythm and blues began its ascent to postwar popularity, New Orleans musicians weren't playing catch-up; they were in the vanguard. The musicians that Dave Bartholomew put together, and Cosimo Matassa recorded, would back up Fats Domino, Little Richard, and Lloyd Price. Ray Charles, in his early days, was drawn to New Orleans, where he played piano on Guitar Slim's hit, "The Things I Used to Do."

Bartholomew would become one of the most important figures in New Orleans music over the next two decades as a bandleader, producer, and arranger. He had fallen in love with music from following the flatbed trucks around as a kid. But when he was able to gain access to a radio, and heard Louis Armstrong for the first time, he had found his calling and instrument. As a boy in the early 1930s, he took lessons from Peter Davis, who had taught Armstrong. Drafted into the army in 1942, he learned how to write and arrange music; his army band played Count Basie arrangements. When he first heard the music of Louis Jordan, it impressed him with its cleverness and its small-group swing sound, which he brought back to New Orleans after the war. He started leading his own group in clubs, dance halls, and church socials, playing his arrangements of Louis Jordan tunes and those of other popular swing bands, and assembling a new generation of New Orleans musicians. "So what I did," he told an interviewer for Boston's WGBH:[1]

> I made it all sound in unison so we'd get a big sound. And everybody in New Orleans was talking about what a great band that is. Then I was lucky enough to get great people like Lee Allen, Alvin "Red" Tyler, the great Earl Palmer, the great Ernest McLean. All my musicians were great because we would rehearse every day, and what actually happened, every day we would come up with something new to make it more rhythmic. And ah, that's what was actually happening was a real good, good beginning for us. Because we could actually feel our music too. And we were drawing all kind of crowds,

at least three or four thousand people on holidays, during the week we would draw maybe a thousand. We were doing very well at that time with the band.

His first recording session, for DeLuxe, featured the nucleus of his rhythm section, bassist Frank Fields and drummer Earl Palmer, along with alto saxophonist Joe Harris. Guitarist Ernest McLean would join for the second session, and by the time Bartholomew signed with Imperial Records and made his first record with Fats Domino, he had assembled his great horn section featuring tenor sax players Lee Allen and Herbert Hardesty and baritone sax player Alvin "Red" Tyler.

The first tune Bartholomew recorded for DeLuxe was Hoagy Carmichael's swing standard "Stardust," but the rest of the session begins to delineate the emerging new sound of New Orleans rhythm and blues. "Dave's Boogie Woogie" and "Bum Mae" are marred by Bartholomew's

Figure 6.1. Dave Bartholomew, bowing on stage, 1977. Photo: Klaus Hiltscher; Creative Commons Attribution-Share Alike 2.0 Generic license.

limitations as a vocalist—a fact that he willingly acknowledged in later interviews—but when they get to the instrumental break, the driving and inventive beat of Palmer and Fields adds new possibilities to Bartholomew's New Orleans brass band–derived trumpet.

Bartholomew's second session for DeLuxe, in 1949, produced "Country Boy," his first minor hit. He again takes the lead vocal, although he was soon to move on past singing to concentrate on writing, arranging, and leading a band. But he also contributes a lengthy trumpet solo, which blends the New Orleans brass band style with Jacquet-influenced honking, or a trumpet version of it.

Los Angeles native Lew Chudd was one of those white entrepreneurs who became aware of the burgeoning and underserved market for the new Black music, and he had heard about New Orleans, an untapped resource. Bartholomew recalled their first meeting in the same WGBH interview:

> He sat around for a week before he said anything to me, because I had come up with quite a few instrumentals that we had just put together and I must say it sounded pretty good . . . Lew said . . . well, what happened Bartholomew, I never did hear this music before. And I said, well, what actually happened, I put it together, you know, just a little ditty and you know, something that swings. So he said, do you think you can get somebody to put a nickel [in the jukebox] on one of your records? So I said, um, I don't know, but I can try. So sure enough, a month later he came to New Orleans, Louisiana and knocked on my door, and said, I'm ready.

Bartholomew took Chudd to a small club in the Ninth Ward, where a young pianist-singer named Fats Domino was playing. Domino was a star in the making, and his first recording for Chudd's Imperial label proved it. The song was "The Fat Man," with Bartholomew's arrangement and Bartholomew's band: Bartholomew (trumpet, arranger); Joe Harris (alto sax); Herbert Hardesty, Clarence Hall (tenor sax); Alvin "Red" Tyler (baritone sax); Ernest McLean (guitar); Frank Fields (bass); and Earl Palmer (drums). Along with a few others, including Lee Allen and pianist James Booker, these were the musicians brought together by Bartholomew to create the New Orleans version of small-group swing. They were to keep the fullness and originality of that sound intact into the rock and roll era.

Because of the presence and extraordinary success of gifted vocalists like native sons Domino, Lloyd Price, Smiley Lewis, and Georgia native Little Richard, all of whom recorded at Cosimo Matassa's New Orleans studios, the musicians assembled by Bartholomew are best known for their work as accompanists. The popularity of the New Orleans artists, and artists who recorded in New Orleans, was so great that the musicians in this relatively small city were kept extremely busy. They can only be heard on a few instrumental pieces.

Kansas-born, Denver-raised Lee Allen came to New Orleans in 1943 to attend Xavier University on a joint athletic and music scholarship. That was one year after Illinois Jacquet's "Flying Home" solo had changed the world for tenor saxophone players. Allen had grown up listening to, and being deeply affected by, the three men who had changed the perception of the instrument: Coleman Hawkins, Lester Young, and Ben Webster. And there was one more tenorman whom Allen listened to and learned from: Joe Thomas, the first saxophone in Jimmie Lunceford's orchestra. Lunceford played a tuneful, melodic style of swing, and Allen came to be known as the most melodic of the young "honker generation" of tenor saxophonists.

Discovered by Paul Gayten while still at Xavier, Allen quickly became one of the mainstays of the studio band at Cosimo Matassa's J&M Studio, as well as spending a lot of time on the road with Fats Domino. His solos on records by Domino and Little Richard are his best known, but some of his other work from that era is worth attention. T-Bone Walker continued to be active throughout the 1940s and '50s, recording for the leading independent labels, including Atlantic and Imperial. His music continued to be his own blend of traditional blues with the melodic inventiveness of Los Angeles swing, without much concession to the rhythm and blues and rock and roll styles of the era. Walker was not making hits for the contemporary audience of Black dancers, and this was way too early for the discovery of the blues greats by white audiences. But the records are there, treasured by collectors even if overlooked in their own time. Imperial sent Walker down to New Orleans in 1953 to record with a nine-piece band led by Dave Bartholomew, and featuring Allen and Herb Hardesty, with satisfying results.

Also in 1953, New Orleans musicians traveled to New York to play on an Atlantic Records session with Joe Turner that produced his hit, "Honey Hush." Allen and Alvin "Red" Tyler appeared with a group led by

Figure 6.2. T-Bone Walker at the American Folk Blues Festival in Hamburg, March 1972. Photo by Heinrich Klaffs. Creative Commons Attribution-Share Alike 2.0 Generic license.

Pluma Davis. Fats Domino is credited as the piano player on the session, but that has been questioned.

Allen's first session as a leader, in 1954, featured a three-horn front line: he was joined by two veterans of the New Orleans traditional jazz style, Joshua "Jack" Willis on trumpet and Waldren "Frog" Joseph on trombone, along with a Bartholomew/Matassa rhythm section including Frank Field on bass and Earl Palmer on drums. The two instrumentals from the session, "The Eel" and "Creole Alley," blend the New Orleans version of small-group swing with the sound of the street bands. The record was released on Savoy. "Creole Alley" would later become a staple of the Bourbon Street strip clubs, a memento of the days when Allen, like many struggling musicians of the era, found work in burlesque houses accompanying strippers—with the musicians hidden behind a screen, so they would not be seen on the same stage as nearly naked white girls.

A 1955 session for Specialty was headed by guitarist-vocalist Roy Montrell, with a rhythm section of Edward Frank (piano), Fields, and Palmer, and the two saxophones of Allen and Tyler. The song is "Every

Time I Hear That Mellow Saxophone," and the title could hardly be more misleading, as Allen and Tyler are given free rein to improvise over an orgiastic beat laid down by Palmer. Perhaps Allen is at his best on another session as leader, with the same rhythm section plus Justin Adams on guitar, this time for Aladdin in 1956. They recorded two tunes, "Shimmy" and "Rockin' at Cosmo's." The latter, presumably a simplified-spelling tribute to Cosimo Matassa and his studio, gives Allen room to improvise over a blues riff with able propulsion from Palmer.

1956 also saw Allen begin working as a producer for New York's Herald/Ember Records, although he was still working out of New Orleans. He recorded his biggest hit, "Walkin' with Mr. Lee," for Ember in 1957. Palmer had by then departed for the West Coast, but Matassa's studio band, and Allen's record, had been augmented by a young keyboardist (here on organ) who would become the most dominant figure in a new generation of New Orleans music: Alan Toussaint. There were a few more sessions for Ember, producing some interesting music. "Cat Walk," co-written by Allen and Toussaint, and "Creole Alley" featured another newcomer to the scene, Mac Rebennack, on guitar. But no more hits. And shortly after this Allen moved to Los Angeles, where, frustrated by his inability to find regular studio work, he retired from music for a number of years. Central Avenue was no longer the mecca it had once been.

Allen returned to performing in the 1970s, being featured on a 1973 album by Big Joe Turner, along with Roy Eldridge on trumpet and Al Grey on trombone. Backing up Turner, the veteran of Prohibition-era Kansas City, with a rhythm section that included Ray Brown on bass and Earl Palmer on drums, and with LP-era room to stretch out for six or seven minutes on a track, Allen contributes the kind of looser, more improvisational solo that one associates with LP-era jazz, as opposed to the tighter limitations of a 78 or 45 RPM single. This session was produced by Norman Granz for Pablo Records; Granz would bring Allen back a decade later for another Turner session, and one with Jimmy Witherspoon, this time pairing Allen with Red Holloway. In a seemingly unusual move for an old New Orleans jazzman, Allen capped his career by joining the Blasters, a Los Angeles rock group led by two brothers, Dave and Phil Alvin. Along with Phil Alvin, he also recorded a 1986 session with the Dirty Dozen Brass Band.

New Orleans native Herb Hardesty was a trumpet prodigy, learning to play on an instrument given to his stepfather by Louis Armstrong, joining Papa Celestin's band in 1939 as a fourteen-year-old, and then receiving an offer from Chick Webb to join his band. When World War II broke out, he lied about his age (sixteen) and joined the Army Air Corps. His first posting was Jackson, Mississippi, where the base band needed a saxophonist and Hardesty volunteered. His commanding officer bought him his first sax, an alto. He learned how to play it in two days and kept it with him as he was posted overseas to Morocco, Italy, and Germany as part of the support team for the Tuskegee Airmen, broadening his musical education by playing with African and European musicians.

By the time he started working regularly with Bartholomew and Matassa, Hardesty was exclusively playing the tenor sax, but when the baritone saxophone player failed to show up for a Fats Domino date, Hardesty volunteered. "Blue Monday" was his first and only occasion to play the baritone sax on record, and his eight-bar solo has such purity and richness of tone that it has rightly been hailed as one of the great solos of the rhythm and blues era.

Hardesty's studio and touring work, especially with Fats Domino, kept him busy, and he did not get to record as a leader until the late 1950s, when the era of small-group swing was pretty much over and the musicians who had followed that path were starting to look in different directions. But his instrumental pieces still carry authority and still swing, especially a few sides he made in New York City with Hank Jones on piano. "Perdido Street" (1959) is particularly worth a listen.

In the 1970s Hardesty moved to Las Vegas, where he showed his versatility by picking up the trumpet again to play briefly in Duke Ellington's orchestra; then he returned to playing the tenor sax to join Count Basie's band (none of this was recorded). As a member of the Hilton Hotel orchestra, he also backed up Tony Bennett, Ella Fitzgerald, and Frank Sinatra. Hardesty played on a 1978 session in LA with Tom Waits; his tenor sax solo can be heard on "Romeo Is Bleeding."

Alvin "Red" Tyler was born and grew up in New Orleans. He recalls going to dances and hearing music as a teenager, where, as he told British author John Broven: "I think my biggest influence to play saxophone was a guy called Sam Lee who played with Sidney Devigne, they had a swing band. Well, I got hooked. I'd go to dances and stand by the bandstand." But it was wartime, and he went into the service at age nineteen and actually picked up the saxophone for the first time to play in a Navy band. Back in his home town after the war, the GI Bill was offering veterans a chance at higher education of all kinds,. It also gave birth to a new music school, started by the Grunewald Music Company, a large local chain of music

Figure 6.3. Alvin "Red" Tyler at New Orleans Jazz & Heritage Festival, 1996. Photo by Sumori. Creative Commons Attribution-Share Alike 4.0 International license.

stores. The Grunewald School of Music, remarkably for New Orleans in that era, accepted both Black and white students.

Tyler had found something he could do and do well. After studying at Grunewald, he played a few dates with a couple of other bands (including one backing blues singer Roy Brown) but quickly won a place in New Orleans' most popular dance band, the Dave Bartholomew Orchestra. Perhaps because of coming to music through the Grunewald School, and not through the streets, marching bands, the clubs, Tyler, more than the other core musicians of the New Orleans rhythm and blues scene, thought of himself as a jazz musician, and some of his fondest memories are of those early Bartholomew days. He told New Orleans music historian Jeff Hannusch: "Dave's band was doing a lot of big band tunes. We used to do stock arrangements on stuff by Dizzy Gillespie, Count Basie, Woody Herman and Jimmie Lunceford—a lot of things that were built around a soloist. The rhythm and blues thing didn't really start until later when we started backing up vocalists. I really think if rhythm and blues hadn't taken off like it did, Dave would have had one of the best swing bands in the country."

Tyler frequently headed up the sessions that employed Bartholomew's musicians, which were frequently head arrangements allowing for a good deal of improvisation. He described the process in an interview for a Tulane University website: "We'd all hang out together, and there would be a certain kind of groove that we could lock into, all of us. That's what made it so easy for us to go into the studio. We could go in, and we'd all know what the concept was, what it was supposed to be." Or, as he told John Broven:

> We'd go into the studio and the guys would say, "what are you going to do?" And the artists would sing the song, the pianists would catch it, the bass would get the thing, Lee Allen and myself would get together and come up with the riff, and we would say "that doesn't lay right," to come up with something else. And we would make the thing up right there, nothing written, so actually we got by without an arrangement fee. Now in a sense that may have been why some of the things were so groovy, they were done how we felt, not how it was written. And a piece of music written can find you to a degree, and if you do it out of your head, either it lays right or it doesn't. If it grooves, it's gonna happen.

Tyler recorded an instrumental album in 1960 that included his version of a 1927 song, "Peanut Vendor" (originally "El Manisero," a Cuban *son* written by Moisés Simons), which later became an important part of the soundtrack of the TV series *Breaking Bad*. In 1961, he joined composer / arranger Harold Battiste in forming the Black collectively owned record label, AFO (All For One) Records. They had an immediate success with Barbara George's "I Know" (featuring a trumpet solo by Melvin Lastie), but their real commitment was to jazz and the new jazz community that was forming in New Orleans. The experiment was to last for two years, until distribution problems forced its shutdown. In 1986 and 1987, Tyler made two albums of straight-ahead jazz for Rounder Records, playing tenor saxophone on original compositions and jazz standards like Billy Strayhorn's "Lush Life."

Between his work in New Orleans and his later career in Los Angeles, Earl Palmer may be the most recorded drummer of his era, and with good reason. Painter Peter Jones, a teenaged jazz fan—and jazz snob—recalls the moment he realized that there was something rich and valuable in this music his younger brother was listening to:

> As a teenager who loved jazz and only jazz, I remember play-ing the start of the 45 of Little Richard's "Slippin' and Slidin'" over and over, marveling at the rhythm. I knew nothing about the musicians then, but when I read about Earl Palmer after moving to Louisiana, I started tracking down his recordings. His New Orleans classics are incredibly good of course, but the same swing is driving "Rockin' Robin" and the other sides he made after moving to California and getting better paid for his genius. What is it about him? His two and four are slightly delayed, giving it a powerful swing. His timing is so accurate that you feel all the other beats.[2]

Palmer was New Orleans–born into a musical family, and his first exposure to performing was as a five-year-old tap dancer with his mother's vaudeville troupe. By twelve he was headlining shows as a dancer. Like Tyler, he took advantage of the GI Bill to enroll in the Grunewald School of Music, studying piano and percussion and learning to read music. And like Tyler, he was hired by Dave Bartholomew for his swing band and brought over by Bartholomew to form the new group he was putting together for Imperial Records, initially to record Fats Domino.

The back beat, the shifting of the accents in a 4/4 measure from the first and third beats, traditionally defined as the strong beats in a mea-sure, to the second and fourth, traditionally thought of as the weak beats, came to define rhythm and blues and particularly rock and roll. "It's got a back beat you can't lose it," Chuck Berry sang. My friend Peter Jones, the teenage jazz snob, pounced on that lyric as we debated the merits of jazz versus rock and roll. He'd say, "That's the problem—you can't lose it no matter how hard you try."

This was also the era in which bebop drummers like Max Roach, Art Blakey, Stan Levey, and particularly Kenny Clarke were virtually reinventing the art of drumming, taking the job of keeping the beat away from the bass drum, operated by a foot pedal, and moving it to the ride cymbal, which was faster, more delicate, more supple. And it was this distinction—the bebop rhythm versus the back beat—that, perhaps more than anything else, caused the critics and tastemakers of the 1940s, and especially the 1950s, to so categorically cast rhythm and blues out of the sacred temple of jazz.

The back beat, like anything else you can name in music—or any other art form—didn't spring fully formed out of nothing. You can trace its origins to the Black Pentecostal church, nurturing ground for so many jazz and rhythm and blues artists. Roy Porter has described how Earl Bostic taught him the double shuffle with a back beat. Roy Milton is credited with—and blamed for—adding a back beat to a boogie-woogie rhythm. But many say that the real back beat started in New Orleans, in Cosimo Matassa's studio, with Fats Domino's first session for Imperial Records, backed by Dave Bartholomew's band featuring Earl Palmer. The song was Domino's reworking of a New Orleans blues about drug addiction, Champion Jack Dupree's "Junker's Blues." To make it more palatable to a larger audience, which was beginning to include white teenagers, the lyrics were rewritten to make it autobiographical for a clean-cut, happy-go-lucky performer: "The Fat Man." It was given a new beat, by Palmer, as he explained: "That song required a strong afterbeat throughout the whole piece. With Dixieland you had a strong afterbeat only after you got to the shout last chorus . . . It was sort of a new approach to rhythm music."

So what brought young Peter Jones, caught up in the intoxicating swell of bebop, rejecter of the back beat that you can't lose, under the spell of Earl Palmer? Much has been made of Palmer's impeccable time, so good as to be metronomic. But that can't be the whole explanation.

There's a story about a sound engineer who was working a session for disco king Nile Rodgers, whose hit record "Le Freak" is considered by many to be the quintessence of disco. This engineer, in a quiet rebellion against what he considered the sterile perfection of Rodgers's production, programmed in a tiny glitch into one of the drum tracks, but buried it so far down in the mix that it couldn't be heard. He had not reckoned on Rodgers's sensitive ear. "What was that?" the master producer demanded. "If I wanted mistakes, I would have hired a real drummer!" Palmer could have given it to him without mistakes. So what was the difference between Palmer and the drum machine? Why is Palmer held in such reverence by real drummers?

Drummer Eric Parker describes swing drumming as "a bit looser, with more breath between the notes." Can that be achieved, while still keeping perfect time? Mark Griffith, writing in *Modern Drummer*, says that Palmer's "pocket playing always found the perfect position between a swung and a straight 8th note, which will forever define the elusive concept of groove." Griffith, in the same article, collected a number of reminiscences about Palmer. Drummer Max Weinberg, of Bruce Springsteen's E Street Band and Conan O'Brien's late night TV band, recalls watching Palmer rehearse for a guest appearance on O'Brien's show:

> Seeing him play live really made his style apparent. He started as a dancer in New Orleans, and I got a chance to watch his feet. If you listen to all the records he played on, particularly the Little Richard and Fats Domino records, he always had what they call that great second-line kind of syncopation in his feet. He literally danced on the pedals. I never saw anybody else's feet look like that when they played. He swung like crazy—everybody knows that—and he rocked like crazy. But his feet had this very light, extremely fluid thing. It was from his dance background.

When Palmer moved to LA, everyone wanted him. By one count, he played on 450 sessions in one year. He was a part of the loose and unofficial group of sought-after session musicians dubbed the Wrecking Crew. Palmer played on sessions from "You've Lost That Lovin' Feeling" to the theme for *The Brady Bunch*. He didn't play a lot of jazz, and it's too bad. It would have been interesting, for example, to see what he might have done with the Basie band. Composer Lalo Schifrin, also recorded by Griffith, had this to say about him:

> I have to tell you why I selected Mr. Palmer to work with me, not only on *Mission: Impossible* but on many other things I did. I was new in California, and I had previously lived in New York City for five years. Dizzy Gillespie brought me from Argentina—I was his pianist, composer, and arranger—and in New York City I discovered a drummer I liked very much, Grady Tate. I got used to working with Grady, and when I came to California I had to find someone who played like him, which was a very special style—that kind of feeling, that kind of intensity and energy.
>
> So I asked around for musicians who played close to the style of Grady Tate, and the grapevine told me to check out Earl Palmer. They were right. He didn't play exactly like Grady, of course, as he had his own personality. But I liked

it and we got along very well. Not only did he record with me, but I took him on tours to Europe and the Middle East.

I started my jazz symphony orchestras with Earl. That's why he played on most of the projects I did at the time of *Mission: Impossible.*

So how do the New Orleans musicians fit in with a discussion of small-group swing of the 1940s and '50s, dismissed by the cognoscenti as rhythm and blues, reconsidered as jazz? With the exception of Earl Palmer's major second career in LA, they were mostly a pretty insular group, staying close to New Orleans. They did not record a lot of instrumental music. Tyler and Allen did some, and Allen even had an instrumental hit with "Walkin' with Mr. Lee." Fats Domino, Professor Longhair, and James Booker recorded piano instrumentals. But this was never a main focus.

Musician/author/archivist Billy Vera recalls Paul Gayten telling him, "New Orleans people are crazy, and they know it, so they're uncomfortable anywhere else. That's why they stay."[3] And that is why, Vera theorizes, "a unique way of playing evolved there." He recalls playing a week in a New Orleans hotel as conductor/guitarist for the Shirelles:

> Bartholomew had the house band, so I got to play with some of those cats for a whole week. It was a very different experience. A solid yet fluid beat that was very comfortable to lay in there with.
>
> The Shirelles' hit, "Everybody Loves a Lover" had been recorded with a New Orleans beat, which none of the northern musicians ever played right. Dave's guys were the first and only time it was right.

New Orleans rhythm and blues was a separate entity from the jazz/small-group swing/rhythm and blues world of the West Coast, Midwest, and East Coast of the 1940s. Although this was not entirely true. By the 1940s, radio and jukeboxes were ubiquitous, to the point where Po' Henry, a traditional bluesman from northern Louisiana in the latter part of the twentieth century, when asked where he learned to play the blues, replied, "John R": the white late-night rhythm and blues disc jockey from WLAC in Nashville, Tennessee. The New Orleans musicians knew about Louis Jordan, Illinois Jacquet, and "The Honeydripper." They knew about Lester Young and Count Basie, and Charlie Parker and Dizzy Gillespie.

Earl Palmer said that his drumming inspiration was Max Roach. Still, they were different.

They knew about the traditional New Orleans jazz musicians of the 1920s, too, but they were different from them. There wasn't much of a connection between Dave Bartholomew's crew of the '40s and '50s and the earlier jazz generations. Except there was. You can hear it in that solid yet fluid beat that Billy Vera felt, that second-line syncopation that Max Weinberg saw in Earl Palmer's feet—New Orleans is a city of jazz, and it's part of everyone who grows up and plays there. Harrison Verrett, guitar and banjo player who worked with Papa Celestin, Kid Ory, and other New Orleans jazz ensembles, and who was Fats Domino's early mentor, described Domino's sound to John Broven as "just old two-beat Dixieland but with rhythm and blues." And the New Orleans rhythm and blues players brought to the table what all the jazz musicians of their era brought: rhythmic syncopation, even if it was anchored by a back beat, improvisation, virtuoso solos, music that swung.

CHAPTER SEVEN

Rock and Roll

There are all sorts of theories about what the first rock and roll record was, or exactly when the rock and roll era began, but it can be safely said that in 1954, when Alan Freed arrived in New York, the rock and roll era was here. Freed had first used the phrase in 1951, when he promoted "Moondog's Rock 'n' Roll Party" in Cleveland, and by 1954, it was an established phenomenon: Bill Haley and the Comets recorded "Rock Around the Clock" in 1954; Elvis Presley made his first records for Sun in Memphis; Little Richard recorded "Tutti Frutti"; and doowop records like the Penguins' "Earth Angel" and the Charms' "Hearts of Stone" showed up on the *Billboard* charts. Perhaps even more significant as the harbinger of a new era, white artists began covering Black rhythm and blues records. The Canadian group the Crew-Cuts, as clean cut as their name, covered "Earth Angel" and the Chords' "Sh-Boom" and had hit records with both. The Fontane Sisters covered "Hearts of Stone." Big band era veteran Georgia Gibbs covered LaVern Baker's Atlantic recording "Tweedle Dee" in a version that followed Jesse Stone's arrangement and Baker's style so closely that Baker sued for plagiarism—and lost, when it was ruled that you can't copyright an arrangement.

What this meant for the musicians playing small-group swing was that any chance they might have had for their music to be taken seriously as an art form, as a genre of jazz, was gone and gone for good. Adults, as a general class, hated rock and roll. Jazz critics and jazz disc jockeys really hated rock and roll. Deejays like Art Ford, Jack Lacey, and William B. Williams—who played what was called "good music" (later labeled "easy listening" or MOR, for "middle of the road") loved the music of the swing era and might even play a little modern jazz—really really really hated rock and roll. So this new musical era was good for the musicians of small-group swing (and even for some progressive jazz musicians) because it gave them work, but it was not so good in that any hope they had of being recognized as serious musicians was gone, beyond redemption.

This is why, as subsequent decades saw the eventual acceptance of jazz as a major American art form, at least a few musicians who had recorded for Blue Note, Prestige, or Impulse! might find themselves hired to head up the jazz department at a college, whereas musicians who had placed hit records on the *Billboard* rhythm and blues charts found themselves playing in shmaltzy hotels or in second-rate resort bands, or out of the music business altogether.

What's interesting is how much the music itself survived. Not only were musicians like Illinois Jacquet, Tiny Bradshaw, Red Prysock, Joe Liggins, and Joe Morris still playing it (Jacquet even made an ill-fated attempt to put together a big band playing classic swing), younger musicians were coming up and playing swing music with the back beat of Roy Milton, Earl Palmer, and Panama Francis, with the ecstatic tenor saxophone solo improvisation of Jacquet, Jack McVea, or Red Prysock (Prysock would have his biggest hit, "Hand Clappin'," in this era). There would still be the occasional hit or near-hit instrumental record, but beyond that, on records by balladeers, shouters, or doowop groups, there would be instrumental breaks that would feature improvisations in the tradition, keeping the flame alive.

The '50s were an odd decade in American music and much less homogeneous than they're remembered as being. Because of the worldwide cultural dominance of rock music in the 1960s and '70s, the '50s are thought of as the decade of rock and roll, but that was not exactly the case. Many radio stations, like New York's popular WNEW, played no rock and roll at all, dedicating themselves to "good music." On other stations that played the newly popular top forty format, a weekly culture war was played out that could rival the War on Christmas or anything else the forces of Qanon might dream up. On the one side, were the rock-and-rollers: Elvis Presley, Buddy Holly, Bill Haley, the white teen idols, and the white performers covering rhythm and blues records (the real rhythm and blues artists were there but often dwarfed on top forty radio—neither Fats Domino nor Chuck Berry nor Little Richard ever had a number one record in the '50s). On the other side, show tunes from contemporary musicals like *The Pajama Game* and new, mostly undistinguished material

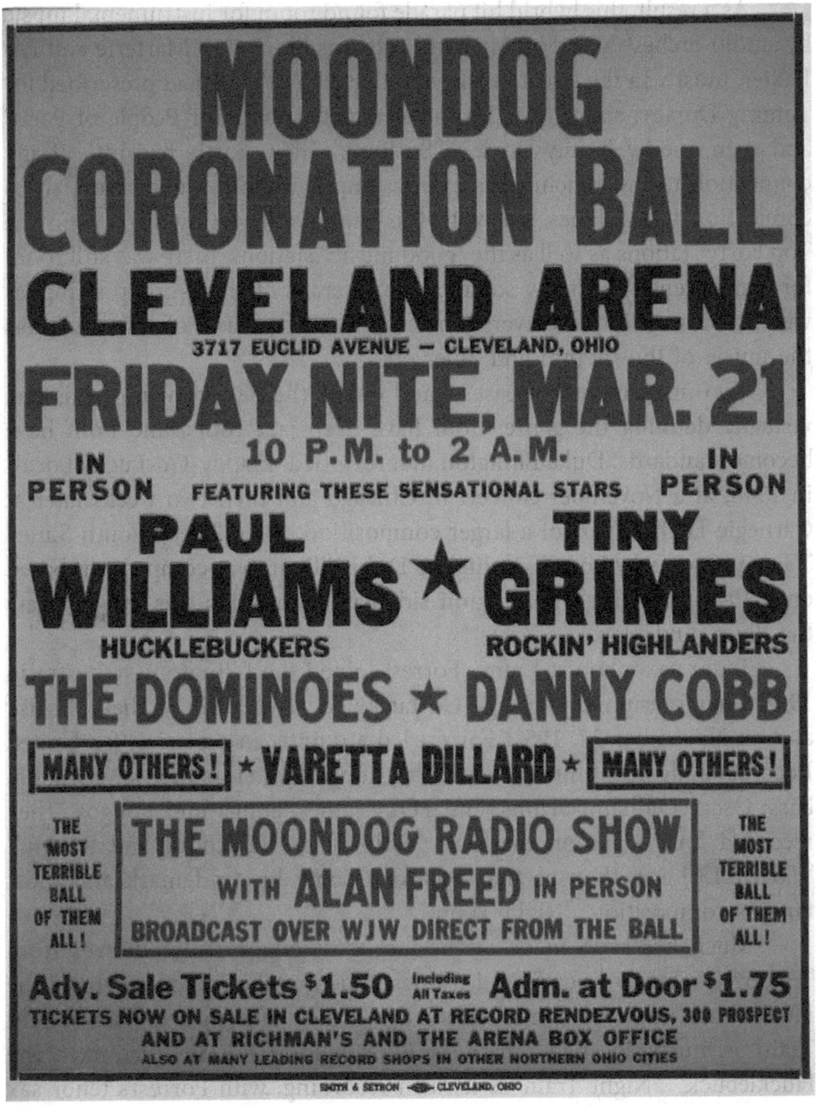

Figure 7.1. Poster for Alan Freed's Moondog Coronation Ball listing jazz and R&B artists, 1952. Public domain.

from the denizens of what was known as Tin Pan Alley—the mythical home of veteran professional songwriters—were sung by big band era veterans like Frank Sinatra or Jo Stafford or younger crooners like Eddie Fisher and Connie Francis.

As a result, this hybrid hit parade found room for instrumental music by studio orchestras led by big band veterans like Ralph Marterie and Les Baxter, mostly in the sweet music vein that RCA Victor had prescribed for Tommy Dorsey: songs like "Lisbon Antigua" and "Poor People of Paris" and even one by Jimmy Dorsey, "So Rare." They mostly had little if any connection to the benchmarks of jazz: improvisation, syncopation, some connection to the blues. But with this music still getting airplay, on the Top Forty stations as well as the "good music" stations, there was still room for instrumental music by some of the veterans of small-group swing, as well as some younger players whose immediate frame of reference was the music of the rhythm and blues era.

Two instrumental releases stand out as the best known of this era, virtually defining the genre. Both have deep jazz roots, and both have become standards. Duke Ellington first recorded "Happy-Go-Lucky Local" in 1946, at a November concert in Chicago and then two weeks later at Carnegie Hall, as part of a larger composition called "Deep South Suite." "Happy-Go-Lucky Local," credited to Duke Ellington as composer, is based on a 1940 recording by Ellington sideman Johnny Hodges titled "That's the Blues, Old Man."

Tenor saxophonist Jimmy Forrest joined the Ellington Orchestra in 1948, when presumably "Happy-Go-Lucky Local" was still on their playlist, and on November 27, 1951, Forrest led a quintet in a session for United Records made up of himself on tenor; Bunky Parker, piano; John Mixon, bass; Oscar Oldham, drums; and Percy James, conga and bongos. They recorded four songs on that day: "Bolo Blues," "Swingin' and Rockin'," "Coach 13," and the one that was to become his trademark and most famous composition, "Night Train."

Much has been made of the fact that "Night Train" derives from "Happy-Go-Lucky Local." And it does, much in the same way that "The Hucklebuck" derives from "Now's the Time," although in fact "Night Train" is much closer to "That's the Blues, Old Man." However, like "The Hucklebuck," "Night Train" is its own recording, with Forrest's tenor sax solo at the center of it, given another dimension by Percy James's conga fills. It had that elusive sound that connects with audiences: a seductive rhythmic groove for dancing, an arresting bravura solo improvisation, and a strong melodic hook. As with "The Hucklebuck," the hook comes from another source, but this is something that was not uncommon in that era, and it's what you do with it that makes a successful record. "Night Train" went to number one on the rhythm and blues charts. A follow-up by the white trombonist and bandleader Buddy Morrow found success on

Billboard's pop charts, with Morrow recreating Forrest's saxophone solo on the trombone. James Brown would later create his own version and have a hit with it. "Night Train" has continued to have a life in the repertoire of pop and jazz groups alike. Oscar Peterson made a particularly lovely recording of it.

Forrest's career was a fluid one, which is to say, he went on making music, which became jazz or rhythm and blues mostly according to the way it was marketed. He was a member of the Jay McShann and Andy Kirk bands before joining Ellington. After the success of "Night Train," he became something of a prisoner of that success, because audiences wanted to hear "Night Train," and record companies, always in pursuit of that elusive hit record, wanted more of the same. His music from the 1950s is captured in a live recording from The Barrel, a nightclub in his hometown of St. Louis. He played there often, but this particular session became noteworthy and was recorded because of the musician who sat in with his combo that night, another hometown cat: Miles Davis, who had left New York in discouragement over the critical and commercial failure of his new sound (later to be heralded as one of the most important recordings of its time when Capitol Records released *Birth of the Cool* in 1957). Davis spent a few years wandering around the Midwest and fighting drug addiction. This club date in St. Louis (the date is given as 1952, but it may have been earlier) was picked up and released several years later by Prestige Records, and recent reviewers have not been kind to it, calling the music "competent but uninspired."

They could not be more wrong, and one suspects that this may be to some extent a conditioned reflex: "Forrest, oh yeah, 'Night Train,' rhythm and blues, how good could he be?" Forrest is playing with his working band, including Mixon and Oldham, two of the musicians who played the "Night Train" date. The album is a piece of living history, jazz as it was, and played by working musicians in small clubs in the Midwest, music that came out of the legacy of the territorial bands of the '20s and '30s, the nighttime wail of America that John Clellon Holmes captured so vividly in his jazz novel *The Horn*. Forrest would later play with the Count Basie orchestra, and he is seen in the 1979 documentary about Basie, *The Last of the Blue Devils*, playing an extended version of "Night Train," after which Basie tells the filmmaker, "The only thing I can say about him—he's just one of the greatest. The most underrated tenor player around."

Bill Doggett, born in 1918, began playing professionally in the swing era. A band that he put together to play gigs around New York was essentially bought out by Lucky Millinder, who was an entrepreneur and impresario rather than a musician, arranger, or conductor, so the Lucky Millinder Orchestra with whom Doggett made his first recordings for Decca in 1938, and which became the featured band at New York's Savoy Ballroom, was essentially Doggett's.

As musical director and arranger for the hit-making Ink Spots in the early 1940s, Doggett was responsible for their sound on a string of hits, including their collaborations with Ella Fitzgerald. He would move on to become Fitzgerald's musical director and arranger for a couple of years. He did the same for Helen Humes on her hit "Be-Baba-Leba," with Wild Bill Moore on tenor sax. Doggett recorded with Cootie Williams (as arranger) and, on piano, with Wynonie Harris, Illinois Jacquet, Lucky Thompson, Buddy Tate, and Johnny Otis. From 1947 to 1951, he was pianist-arranger for Louis Jordan, sharing that job with Wild Bill Davis. Jordan's popularity was such that he was booked all the time, and needed new material all the time, so while Davis went out on the road with the band, Doggett would work on new arrangements. Then they would reverse roles, Doggett playing with the band, Davis at home writing arrangements. Davis eventually moved on, and Doggett became arranger and musical director for one of the nation's most popular bands.

Davis had gotten fascinated by the Hammond B3 organ and had formed one of the first jazz organ trios. Doggett kept in touch with his old bandmate and started realizing the possibilities of the organ too. When he left Jordan to form his own group, it was as an organist. His first recorded appearance on organ came in 1949, co-leading a group with Eddie "Lockjaw" Davis for King Records and featuring John Simmons on bass and Jo Jones on drums, presaging the organ-saxophone sound that was to become so popular a decade later. The recording was a smutty novelty tune, "Mountain Oysters," but the organ-saxophone breaks are wild and joyful. Throughout the 1950s, as Doggett continued to specialize on the organ, he continued to be in demand. There are sessions with Paul Quinichette, Coleman Hawkins, Ella Fitzgerald (including a version of "Crying in the Chapel," a song originally marketed as rhythm and blues), and with "Lockjaw" in 1952 for Roost Records, this one with Oscar Pettiford and Shadow Wilson, performing standards and a blues. That same year he recorded one song, "Lonesome and Blue," as a rhythm and blues outing with Big John Greer and again as a straight-ahead jazz recording with Billy Taylor and Stan Getz.

Also in 1952, Doggett was brought in by Henry Glover as a full member of the King Records team and began recording under his own name. Early on, he started working with drummer Shep Shepherd, who had worked with Benny Carter and Artie Shaw, among others. Guitarist Billy Butler, another in-demand session musician who worked with Dizzy Gillespie, Benny Goodman, and Johnny Hodges joined Doggett in 1955, and tenor saxophonist Clifford Scott joined later the same year. Doggett's King records seem to have found an audience, because he kept making them and kept developing his organ sound, as Wild Bill Davis was developing his. The two of them, each in his own way and without knowing, were laying the groundwork for a whole new era of jazz.

Doggett began extending the sound beyond that of the organ trio, building on what he had begun with Eddie Davis and Paul Quinichette. Before hiring Scott, he had made several records with tenor saxophonist Percy France, who would go on to work with Jimmy Smith on one of Smith's most important albums, *Home Cookin'*. Sonny Rollins, who grew up with France in Harlem's San Juan Hill neighborhood, considered him "probably the best player around" during the time that the two of them were starting to make their reputations. But it was with Clifford Scott that Doggett's sound really came together. Scott's background was mostly with the music that was marketed as rhythm and blues, playing with Amos Milburn, Jay McShann, Roy Milton, and Roy Brown. He had also toured with the remarkable big band that Lionel Hampton took to Europe in 1953, with Quincy Jones and Gigi Gryce as arrangers, and featuring such modern jazz giants as Art Farmer and Clifford Brown.

On June 16, 1956, Doggett's band entered the studio to record three tunes: "Hand in Hand," "On the Sunny Side of the Street," and an original tune, "Honky Tonk," which was too long for one side of a 78 or 45 RPM record, so it was split into two parts (the second of which is described in the session log as a bossa nova!). "Honky Tonk" made this jazz veteran into a rock and roll household name and became King Records' all-time best seller. It is a tightly arranged piece of music, with apparently not much room for improvisation, but it was born out of the most casual improvisation imaginable. According to Andrew Hickey in his *A History of Rock Music in 500 Songs* podcast:

> "Honky Tonk, Parts 1 and 2" came about almost by accident. As Doggett told the story, his biggest hit started out at a dance in Lima, Ohio on a Sunday night. The group were playing their normal set and people were dancing as normal, but then in between songs Billy Butler . . . just started noodling an instrumental line on his bass strings:

This hadn't been planned—he was just noodling around, as all guitarists will do when given five seconds silence. But the audience started dancing to it . . . the rest of the group fell in with the riff he was playing, and he started soloing over them:

After three choruses of this, Butler nodded to Clifford Scott . . . to take over, and Scott started playing a honking saxophone version of what Butler had been playing.

After Scott played through it a few times, he looked over to Doggett to see if Doggett wanted to take a solo too. Doggett shook his head. The song had already been going about five minutes and what Butler and Scott had been playing was enough. The group quickly brought the song to a close using a standard blues outro.

And that would have been the end of that. It's the kind of thing that bar bands have jammed a million times, the sort of thing that if you're a musician you think nothing of . . . But then, a couple of songs later, someone in the audience came up and asked them if they could play that hot new song again.

They played it again, as best they could remember it . . . and then again and again, as the dancers kept requesting it. By the end of the night they had played it ten times, and Doggett had phoned Syd Nathan at King to tell him they had a hit. As befits a group effort, the song's composition is credited to Doggett, Butler, Scott, Shepherd, and Henry Glover, King's head of production. As late as 1990, Shepherd told an interviewer that his share of the royalties was still paying his phone bill.

"Honky Tonk" not only dominated the rhythm and blues charts, it went to number two on the pop charts. It gave Doggett name recognition he had never had before and a groove he was not to escape from for the rest of the decade. But by 1962, as music had moved on, he was reunited with Ella Fitzgerald, and they made an album together, *Rhythm Is My Business*. No one much noticed that it was Bill Doggett the rock and roller, a title that had never settled comfortably on Doggett's shoulders, although he not only liked the money, he was proud of the record. "Honky Tonk" was a feature of all his club, concert, and festival dates until his death in 1996. "I just wouldn't be Bill Doggett if I didn't play 'Honky Tonk,'" he would say.

Although Doggett never took an organ solo on "Honky Tonk," the organ was starting to become a significant instrument in the jazz/rhythm and blues orbit as the 1950s progressed. Wild Bill Davis, whose career path had paralleled Doggett's in many ways, also released 45 RPM singles to the jukebox and rhythm and blues market, without having Doggett's breakout success, but in many ways he was a more important influence. Young Jimmy Smith, on first hearing Davis play in 1955, was motivated to take up the organ. And Davis almost had a hit. He had written an arrangement of "April in Paris" for the Count Basie orchestra but wasn't able to show up for the gig. Basie himself (who had learned to play the organ from Fats Waller) took over Davis's organ part, and the result was one of Basie's most enduring hits (number eight on *Billboard*'s rhythm and blues chart).

There were hit records like "The Happy Organ" by Dave "Baby" Cortez that had no jazz roots (although Cortez would occasionally work with jazz musicians). But others, notably Doc Bagby, were solidly within the small-group swing tradition. Henry "Doc" Bagby was from Philadelphia, which seems to have been a breeding ground for jazz organists. He recorded with Tiny Grimes and Panama Francis, then succeeded Doggett in Eddie "Lockjaw" Davis's saxophone-organ combo and played a similar role with saxophonist Sil Austin. Bagby led his own group, featuring, at various times, Seldon Powell on saxophone, Mickey Baker on guitar, Milt Hinton on bass, and Gus Johnson on drums. It was this group, minus Powell and with Ellsworth Gooding on tenor sax, who went into the studio for Columbia subsidiary Okeh Records on January 29, 1957, to make what Columbia hoped would rival "Honky Tonk." Bagby's record, following in the steps of 1940s hits like Hal Singer's "Corn Bread" and Frank Culley's "Cole Slaw," got a soul food title, "Dumplin's." There would never be another "Honky Tonk," but "Dumplin's" and its flip side, "Sylvia's Calling," both did well, and both were good examples of the organ/ saxophone/guitar sound.

The organ also became part of the arsenal of the musician who virtually flattened the distinction between rhythm and blues and jazz, Ray Charles. Charles, who had grown up enthralled by the swing of Artie Shaw, who had embraced the piano jazz and vocal stylings of Nat "King" Cole and Charles Brown, had finally, in the mid-1950s, found his own style, a blend of swing and gospel that no one had ever heard before. It indelibly changed American music, just as Louis Armstrong and Charlie Parker—yes, and Illinois Jacquet—had done years earlier.

Charles created his new style it in the middle of the rock and roll revolution, during a time when his label, Atlantic Records, was putting most of its effort behind creating a catalog of music aimed at the new multiracial youth market that was developing. Charles's first album for Atlantic was entitled *Rock and Roll*, and although his music was anything but, he was still a pariah to the jazz disc jockeys and record reviewers. Atlantic wasn't entirely successful in marketing him as a pop/rock and roll star—his 1959 release "What'd I Say?" was his only 45 RPM single for that label to crack *Billboard*'s top ten. But his talent, his vision, and his importance as a musician were inescapable. Charles finally broke the jazz barrier in 1961 with his album *Genius + Soul = Jazz*, with arrangements by Quincy Jones and Ralph Burns, and a big band composed of Count Basie veterans and other top New York jazz musicians, on which he played both piano and organ.

But Charles had also kept the flame of small-group swing alive on his many rhythm and blues records for Atlantic, in the way that other musicians did, during the rock and roll era: with improvised solos, generally on the tenor saxophone, during the instrumental break in the middle of big-beat vocal numbers aimed at the rhythm and blues or rock and roll markets.

We've seen how the New Orleans recordings of the 1950s, featuring Lee Allen, Herb Hardesty, and Alvin "Red" Tyler, did this. And it was

Figure 7.2. Ray Charles in 1968. Photo: Eric Koch for Anefo. Creative Commons CC0 1.0 Universal Public Domain Dedication.

happening in New York, too. New York by this time had replaced Los Angeles and the dying Central Avenue scene as the rhythm and blues capital of America, as it also become the jazz capital. This meant it was the home of many musicians who, whether they were marketed one way or the other, were all part of one of the greatest concentrations of musical talent the world has ever known.

The tenor saxophone players who filled this role in Charles's band included Sam "the Man" Taylor, Don Wilkerson, David "Fathead" Newman, Cecil Payne, and Hank Crawford. Of these, Newman is probably the most celebrated for his work with Charles, and he would also win acclaim in his later career as a straight-ahead jazz musician. Newman was from Texas and is frequently cited as one of the "Texas tenors": musicians who came from or had ties to that state, who grew up listening or playing with the territory bands, and developed a robust, bluesy, energetic style of play. Illinois Jacquet and Arnett Cobb are generally credited with being the progenitors of the style.

Newman first met Charles when they were both starting out in California. When Charles signed with Atlantic, Newman came onboard as baritone saxophonist, augmenting Don Wilkerson, another Texas tenor (although born in Louisiana). Wilkerson would move on to play with Cannonball Adderley and later to record for Blue Note Records in partnership with guitarist Grant Green. Newman then stepped into the tenor chair. Charles was creating a new sound and always knew exactly what he wanted. Newman's solos on Charles's Atlantic recordings are short—sometimes as short as eight bars—but always perfectly placed and distinctive enough to make people listen and take notice. He was rewarded with a Charles-produced LP, *Fathead: Ray Charles Presents David Newman*, which should once and for all have erased the gap between what was called jazz and what was called rhythm and blues, if the mindset had not been so firmly entrenched. Newman would go on making straight-ahead jazz (and getting a 1990 Grammy nomination) for another four decades.

Thanks to the success of "Honky Tonk Part 2," other saxophone-led records followed, aimed at the pop charts as well as the rhythm and blues charts. One of the most successful was "Slow Walk," released on Mercury by Sil Austin. Austin had first recorded for Mercury on June 5, 1956, as a member of Buddy Johnson's band, backing Johnson's sister Ella. The two had been consistent sellers in the race records/rhythm and blues market since the early 1940s. On the same day, the band, minus the Johnsons, recorded two songs under Austin's name. Then on September 4, Austin brought a quintet, including Doc Bagby and Mickey Baker, for a session that included "Slow Walk," which would go to number three on the *Billboard* rhythm and blues chart and seventeen on the pop chart. This would be followed by two longer sessions in October, with sought-after jazz bassist Wendell Marshall and drummer Jimmy Crawford, veteran of the Jimmie Lunceford band—described as "a key factor in establishing the unique Lunceford beat"—joining the group. In 1958, Austin would be joined by fellow Mercury recording artist Red Prysock for an LP that featured such jazz sidemen as Kenny Burrell, Milt Hinton, and Panama Francis.

A versatile player, Austin never lacked for work. He was also open to exploring additional styles, which led to success in a totally different genre, as he told an interviewer:

> Mercury had Clyde Otis, and David Carroll and these guys got together and decided, "This guy's got such great tone, suppose we put strings and voices behind him." Man, it changed my sound. They had strings from the New York Philharmonic, the Ray Charles Singers, and low and behold the sound sold. That's when they stopped concentrating on the "Slow Walk" sound and on singles. I started doing theme albums—*Sil Austin Plays Pretty Melodies From Around the World, Sil Austin Plays Folk Tunes* . . . I didn't mind the change, because the albums were selling. All the honkers weren't gettin' much and I was gettin' paid pretty good.
>
> I ended up being one of the most recorded saxophonists of my generation. Thirty-two albums; probably more. I lost count. My stuff comes out in parts of the world I only hear about later on. I got to do things with strings and orchestras, the New York Philharmonic; all the voices I wanted, whatever. Mercury put everything at my disposal. They knew I was gonna be good.

Other tenor saxophonists, some younger than the swing era veterans but with the same commitment to a danceable, blues-oriented, accessible form of jazz, also found record labels interested in seeing if they could capture the "Honky Tonk" magic and some of the "Honky Tonk" dollars. One such was Noble "Thin Man" Watts, who signed with the small independent New York label Baton and had some success with "Hard Times (The Slop)." The tune, composed by Watts, had first been recorded by Dave Bartholomew in February 1957, leading a New Orleans band that featured Lee Allen and Herb Hardesty, but Watts's version was released first.

Watts's story is illustrative of the life of a rhythm and blues musician. Born in DeLand, Florida, in 1926, he raked leaves on the campus of Stetson University in his home town in exchange for violin lessons, then went to Florida A&M, where he played in the marching band along with the Adderley brothers. Nat Adderley remembered him as having, at first, a lot of talent but not much formal training, but "he expanded his musical knowledge by learning to read music, by learning chord progressions and harmony and composition." That training stood him in good stead when in 1951 he joined a band led by the Griffin Brothers, Juilliard graduates who led a popular rhythm and blues band in the Washington, DC, area. He worked with Paul Williams and Amos Milburn in the early 1950s.

There were no more hits after "Hard Times," and Watts's career sank. In the 1980s, a young musician named Bob Greenlee was amazed to discover the tenor sax soloist of "Hard Times" playing in a third-rate lounge band in Central Florida. Greenlee had his own independent label and recorded a comeback album by Watts, *The Return of the Thin Man*, in 1987, featuring a guest appearance by blues and Americana star Taj Mahal. Watts was one of the lucky ones. His contribution to American music was belatedly recognized. He received an honorary doctorate in 2000 from Stetson, and the African American Museum of the Arts dedicated an amphitheater named after Watts in his hometown. In a late interview, he said, "I like to feel I'm leaving a mark in the form. I'd like for it to be that when I die, my music don't die with me. I'd like for somebody to say, 'I got a lot out of what Noble did. He left a lot for us to go on.'"

Some excellent examples of the improvised music made by the heirs to the small-group tradition can be found in what might be thought of as unlikely places—the instrumental breaks to rhythm and blues and rock and roll songs. Perhaps the earliest of these can be found on first doowop song to hit the *Billboard* pop chart top ten—the Chords' version of "Sh-Boom." This rhythm and blues hit was eclipsed by a white Canadian group, the Crewcuts, who covered the song with the bland, easy-listening accompaniment of the David Carroll orchestra. But the Chords' original version had a thirty-two-bar tenor sax solo by a veteran of the Cootie Williams, Cab Calloway, and Lucky Millinder bands. Sam "the Man" Taylor would go on to be one of the most sought-after session men of the 1950s, lending his honking tenor improvisations to countless rhythm and blues and rock and roll hits and leading the band that performed at disc jockey Alan Freed's stage shows. Among Taylor's most remarkable credits was his tenor sax accompaniment to Langston Hughes reading his poetry on a 1958 LP.

One of the most significant—and most obscure—of the era's tenor sax stylists was Jimmy Wright, who led the various bands backing up recording acts for New York independent labels Gee and Rama. They mostly specialized in the city's indigenous doowop singing groups, such as the Valentines, the Cleftones, and most prominently, Frankie Lymon and the Teenagers. The young singers and harmonizers, many of whom were very good, were also very untrained, and the sound of a record depended to a considerable extent on the musicians hired for the date. Most of the musicians who played on sessions for New York's indie labels were jazz musicians who were glad to have a payday, but that didn't mean they were just "phoning it in," just going through the motions on these sessions. The musicians that Wright hired for the Teenagers' "Why Do Fools Fall in Love?" were guitarist Jimmy Shirley, whose extensive résumé included work with Ella Fitzgerald, Billie Holiday, and Coleman Hawkins; bassist Al Hall, who worked for many years with Errol Garner; and Gene Brooks, a blues drummer whose recorded credits include work with Lucille Hegamin and Sonny Terry/Brownie McGhee. Wright's solos enrich the vocal performance of young Lymon and his cohorts, and they stand up on their own.

Wright did record a few instrumental pieces under his own name, but they never got much airplay or sales. They're not bad, but his solos and arrangements on the Gee/Rama doowop instrumental breaks are really his best recorded work. Someone has gone to the trouble of editing his solos on the Teenagers' records together and posting them on YouTube, and it's worth a listen.

Remarkably little is known about Wright, but he was a New York jazz veteran by the time he hooked up with, and quickly became the de facto musical director for, Gee and Rama Records. He had played with Thelonious Monk in the 1940s—one recording of Wright with Monk and Hot Lips Page exists on a hard-to-find CD compiled from tapes of sessions at Minton's Playhouse in Harlem. It is known that he lived in Europe for a while, then returned to New York. Billy Vera reports, "When I had the house band in a 1972 oldies show at New York's Academy of Music on 14th Street, we had the Teenagers, Cleftones, and Valentines, and Jimmy called me, saying he remembered all his solos. I begged the promoter to hire him for the authenticity, but he refused. Broke my heart."

Buddy Lucas, known for his prowess on harmonica as well as tenor saxophone, worked with Horace Silver and Yusef Lateef. In the 1960s, his range brought him recording dates with funkster Jimmy Smith and avant-gardist Albert Ayler. During the 1950s, he filled much the same role for Gone/End Records that Wright filled with Gee/Rama (both companies were owned by the same entrepreneur, George Goldner). Lucas's "7-11," a rhythm and blues interpretation of Perez Prado's "Mambo #5," credited to the Gone All-Stars, was a successful record and is most representative of Lucas's work.

A few other saxophone solos deserving mention on records by rhythm and blues vocalists: Jesse Powell on "Speedoo" by the Cadillacs, "Since I Met You Baby" by Ivory Joe Hunter, and "Mr. Lee" by the Bobbettes; Sam "the Man" Taylor on "When You Dance" by the Turbans, "Tweedle Dee" and "Jim Dandy" by LaVern Baker.

On the West Coast, the most prominent tenor saxophone player to straddle both the jazz and rhythm and blues worlds was Louisiana-born Plas Johnson, who left no genre untouched. He was discovered in the late 1940s by Paul Gayten; then, on moving to Los Angeles, he began working with Charles Brown in 1951. Maxwell Davis, a leading West Coast tenor player who became much better known as a producer, began hiring Johnson for his productions. Johnny Otis, then working for Capitol, hired Johnson, who was soon playing behind Nat "King" Cole, Peggy Lee, and Frank Sinatra, while at the same time providing rhythm and blues accompaniment for the Platters and Larry Williams, rock and roll for Ricky Nelson, and jazz partnerships with Chet Baker and Benny Carter. He was the man Henry Mancini wanted for what became Johnson's—and Mancini's—best known saxophone solo: "The Pink Panther."

But the most prominent, and most admired, of the saxophone players to gain prominence in the 1950s working with singers and vocal groups was Curtis Ousley, known professionally as King Curtis. Texas-born, he fit easily into what had become a widely used descriptor of a style, and which, by chance or design, really did fit a lot of young musicians from the region: the Texas tenor. He had first displayed that sound as a member of Lionel Hampton's road band, filling the chair that had previously been occupied by Illinois Jacquet and Arnett Cobb. He then came to New York, where for a while he led the house band at Harlem's famed jazz club Small's Paradise. He recorded with various blues and jazz singers, working often with the musicians who were bringing the styles and voicings of swing to rhythm and blues: Sam Taylor, Mickey Baker, etc. His first recording session as leader paired him with trumpeter Jonah Jones, whose jazz renditions of Broadway show tunes would soon make him one of the hottest selling musicians in jazz, if not necessarily a critics' darling.

In 1957, King Curtis came to Atlantic Records to play on a session with singer Chuck Willis, under the direction of Jesse Stone. He caught the attention of Stone and label president Ahmet Ertegun, who gave him a session of his own in June of 1958, which produced a searing version of "Birth of the Blues." Ertegun then recommended him to songwriters/producers Jerry Lieber and Mike Stoller, who really knew how to harness his talent. His first solo, on the Coasters' record of "Yakety Yak," had people talking as much about the new saxophone in town as about the hugely popular singing group or the high-riding, endlessly clever songwriting team.

~

What was the big difference between the musicians of the 1950s who were classified as jazz and those who were classified as rhythm and blues? Many jazz purists will tell you that it was the simplistic and repetitive harmonic structure of rhythm and blues, compared to the complexity of jazz. But by the middle of the decade, bebop with all its complexity was giving way to what came to be called hard bop, which featured a more danceable rhythm section, and riff-based, frequently blues-based melodies. It can be argued that in the 1950s, the real difference between jazz and rhythm and blues was length.

Jazz was an LP music, R&B was tailored to 45 RPM singles, to the jukeboxes, the radio DJs whose audiences were used to that three-minute format. That meant that an R&B instrumental number was built almost entirely around the main solo instrument, be it saxophone, guitar, piano, organ, or even harmonica. With extended improvisation and with solo space given to every member of the ensemble, a jazz tune can easily go eight to ten minutes or longer. Obviously, this creates a whole different dynamic.

"Honky Tonk" was over five minutes long but broken up into two parts. As Billy Butler had improvised for a couple of minutes the first night he played his riff for dancers, then turned it over to Clifford Scott for his couple of minutes, and as Bill Doggett had declined to take a turn, deciding enough was enough, so it went when it came time to record the number. And so it went when the record went out to the jukeboxes and the disc jockeys, and so it went when "Honky Tonk, Part 2," not "Honky Tonk," hit the charts.

What if, instead of going into King Records studio in Cincinnati, with Henry Glover handling production, jazz veteran Bill Doggett had been signed with Blue Note, and he and his quintet had ended up at Rudy Van Gelder's recording studio in Englewood Cliffs, New Jersey, with Alfred Lion producing the session? How would "Honky Tonk" have gone? Perhaps it might have started with a "head," with Doggett and Scott playing the opening riffs in unison. Then Butler's solo, then Scott's. Then a short bridge by Doggett and a bass solo by Carl Pruitt (he could have contributed an interesting line—listen to his work, from the same period, on Rahsaan Roland Kirk's *Triple Threat* album), followed by a drum solo from Shep Shepherd, then Doggett comes in with a longer organ solo, followed by a restatement of the head, and it's nine minutes on one side of an LP. It wouldn't have become a jukebox hit like "Honky Tonk, Part 2," but it could well have become another "Sidewinder," the Lee Morgan favorite.

CHAPTER EIGHT

Jazz with a Beat

In 1949, nineteen-year-old Bob Weinstock started a record label, Prestige, to record the new genre of music he had fallen in love with: bebop. In 1972, he would sell the label and retire from the music business, having decided that the music he loved was no longer being made. In the interim, in 1959, he started a subsidiary to Prestige called Swingville to record an older generation of musicians who were still active but now largely overlooked: Coleman Hawkins, Buddy Tate, Buck Clayton, and PeeWee Russell. The music they made had the appeal of swing, but it was not just a rehash of records they had made in 1938. It was newer and fresher, made by musicians who knew what had happened in the past decade and a half but still chose to make the music they wanted to make.

Swingville did not include the musicians who had created a new form of small-group swing called rhythm and blues. But in 1961, Weinstock announced a new label, Tru-Sound, which he said would highlight what he called "contemporary rhythm and blues"—perhaps the first recognition by a card-carrying member of the jazz establishment that rhythm and blues was a form of jazz. And the artist most prominently presented by Tru-Sound was King Curtis.

Curtis had already been featured on a few Prestige albums. On April 21, 1960, Prestige producer Ozzie Cadena brought him into Rudy Van Gelder's studio with a powerful lineup of musicians: Nat Adderley on trumpet, Wynton Kelly on piano, Paul Chambers on bass, and Oliver Jackson on drums. In his liner notes, Nat Hentoff tries to come to grips with a rhythm and blues player invading the sacred turf of jazz by invoking Curtis's "driving, functional swing," which is an adjective I hadn't thought of. "Functional" swing? Gets the job done, without really being inspired? Well, that's subjective, but if it's faint praise, that's better than no praise at all, and in fact Hentoff is generally appreciative of Curtis's playing. Curtis himself, quoted by Hentoff, characterizes this album as all jazz, as opposed to the "60 to 70 percent jazz" that his combo customarily plays, again paying tribute, or perhaps lip service, to the supposed unbridgeable gulf between rhythm and blues and jazz.

According to the liner notes, Chambers had played with Curtis before, and here on the nearly eleven-minute version of Curtis's composition "In a Funky Groove," he contributes something you don't find on every funky groove: a bowed bass solo. The album, entitled *The New Scene of King Curtis*, was released on Prestige subsidiary New Jazz, an odd choice in that New Jazz was generally the label of choice for more avant garde, less commercially viable music. A second Nat Adderley session saw Sam Jones on bass and Belton Evans on drums.

As with Swingville, Prestige on its Bluesville subsidiary presented traditional blues singers in a slightly more modern setting, recorded in a better studio (Rudy Van Gelder's), and frequently with jazz accompanists. Curtis played on sessions with Al Smith, Roosevelt Sykes, Sunnyland Slim, Ernestine Allen, and Arbee Stidham. And on Tru-Sound, they even released an album of Curtis himself singing the blues.

An album called *Soul Battle* presents an interesting front line of tenor saxophonists: Oliver Nelson, with impeccable jazz credentials even to the purest of the purists; Jimmy Forrest, with jazz credentials shaded a bit by guilt by association to rhythm and blues; and King Curtis, with rhythm and blues credentials now complicated by his jazz associations. In other words, three cats who could blow the tenor saxophone, blowing together. Or as Tom Wilson (whose credits as a producer range from Sun Ra to Bob Dylan) said in his liner notes: "The three saxophonists represent a subtle gradation of several important styles which have reached full development since 1940, affecting or being affected by the bop revolution." Thank you, Tom Wilson.

The Tru-Sound albums mostly featured Curtis's own band, a tight aggregation, and leaned toward music for dancing, as emphasized by the titles: *Old Gold* (which included "Honky Tonk," "The Hucklebuck," "Harlem Nocturne," "Night Train," and "Soft"), *It's Party Time with King Curtis*, and *Doing the Dixie Twist*. Tru-Sound folded, and Curtis moved on just a little too soon for Bob Weinstock's bank balance. He moved to the smaller Enjoy label and had his breakout hit: "Soul Twist."

The new sound in jazz was coming. In 1959, Ornette Coleman released *The Shape of Jazz to Come,* and in 1960, John Coltrane released *Giant Steps.* But the other new sound, the one that would be hailed as "soul jazz," had started even earlier. In 1956, Eddie "Lockjaw" Davis, who had explored the Hammond organ/tenor saxophone sound as early as 1949, got together with a rising young organist named Shirley Scott for a series of sessions in 1956 and 1957, which would be released by King Records as *Jazz with a Beat.* King credited the album to Davis, "his tenor saxophone and trio," and the four original compositions, which must have been by the two of them (one is named "Scotty Boo") are simply credited to Jay & Cee. This genre of jazz, the organ-saxophone combo, riff-based, funky, a whole new direction in small-group swing, would be developed and expanded on by some new jazz masters in the decade to come, but it's all right there in this first collaboration between a wily veteran and a brilliant twenty-two-year-old making her recording debut.

Figure 8.1. Jimmy Smith, 1958 publicity photo. Public domain.

That same year, there was more jazz with a beat, and another organ debut, by the performer who was destined to become the biggest and most honored star of the new organ-centered soul jazz: Jimmy Smith. And Smith's stardom-in-the-making was immediately apparent to the label that had signed him. Blue Note titled his 1956 debut, which also featured guitarist Thornel Schwartz (who would go on to work with several of the new organists) *A New Sound . . . A New Star . . .* Smith more than lived up to the hype. Already thirty when he signed with Blue Note, he had had time to develop a mature style, inspired by Wild Bill Davis but very much his own. His National Endowment for the Arts citation as an NEA Jazz Master (in 2005) describes his innovative approach to the instrument: "Inspired by the great horn players of the day—Don Byas, Arnett Cobb, Coleman Hawkins—as well as by pianists Art Tatum, Erroll Garner, and Bud Powell, he cut the tremolo off and began playing horn lines with his right hand. He also created a new organ registration to simulate Garner's sound, establishing the standard for jazz organists who would follow."

Smith's appearance at the 1957 Newport Jazz Festival consolidated his reputation and served notice that soul jazz, and the organ, were here to stay. After some forty sessions with Blue Note, where he worked with Kenny Burrell, Lou Donaldson, Jackie McLean, Wes Montgomery, Lee Morgan, Ike Quebec, and Stanley Turrentine, among others, he moved to Verve, where collaborations with big band arrangers Oliver Nelson and Lalo Schifrin added new dimensions to his music. It's an oversimplification to say that rhythm and blues began with Illinois Jacquet, but there's a good deal of truth in that statement. And if one made the same claim for Jimmy Smith with respect to soul jazz, that would be an oversimplification too, but not without some truth.

Shirley Scott would get more recognition with her second Eddie Davis collaboration. This time jazz with a beat would have the sponsorship of the bandleader who had brought Kansas City swing to the Big Apple in impresario John Hammond's 1938 Carnegie Hall Spirituals to Swing concert, and had brought the Big Beat to the Brooklyn Paramount as the bandleader for Alan Freed's first New York stage show. *Count Basie Presents the Eddie Davis Trio + Joe Newman* came out in 1958 on Roulette Records, featuring the Count himself on piano and his star soloist on trumpet. Barry Ulanov, one of the architects of those early definitions of jazz that excluded rhythm and blues, had this to say about the young organist: "Little Shirley Scott is an astonishing musician. She has a big man's power at the manuals and pedals. As the stentor pours force and the rhythmic impulse gathers force, one finds it hard to believe that this girl weighs, at most, one hundred pounds. But the power, effective as it is, is not Shirley's most compelling contribution. It is rather, I think, the surrealist touches with which she decorates the ballads."

Ulanov is very much on target. Scott's "surrealist touches" are explorations of all the possible ways that organ can add to the vocabulary of sound that can make up jazz music. Jazz with a beat was much more than just the beat. Davis and Scott came to Prestige in 1958, recording several albums, beginning with the popular *Eddie "Lockjaw" Davis Cookbook*. Scott then married Blue Note soul jazz artist Stanley Turrentine, and the two of them recorded together for both labels—under her name for Prestige, his for Blue Note. New musicians like Shirley Scott were creating this new sound and so were older veterans of the small-group swing era, like Eddie Davis, and for that matter Wild Bill Davis, who never stopped making records, well into the twenty-first century.

The organ had begun to grow in popularity because musicians like Davis, Doggett, and Smith had shown what it could do, but there was another reason why groups started to use them—a budgetary reason. The organ could do the job of a bass, which meant one less musician would have to be paid, and the sound could be a lot more dynamic. A piano trio mostly had to be piano, bass, and drums. With an organ, you could add a saxophone or an electric guitar and still only be paying three salaries.

One veteran who figured that out was Willis "Gator Tail" Jackson. Without a record label after being dropped by King, he continued playing, working with guitarist Bill Jennings, who had been with him on his last King sessions, and convincing a young bass player he had hired to take up the organ. The bass player's name was Jack McDuff. Gator's new group drew the attention of Prestige producer Esmond Edwards, who had figured out pretty quickly that the new soul jazz was an extension of the small-group swing that had been marketed for years as rhythm and blues and played by veterans like Jackson. Edwards was one of the very few African American producers working for a jazz label. He knew parts of New York, particularly of Harlem, that other producers did not, and he knew about the old Gator and this hot new trio he had assembled. They made their first album for Prestige in 1959, adding the salaries of a bass player (Tommy Potter) and drummer (Alvin Johnson).[1] McDuff began his own career as leader the following year and would go on to one of the most successful careers in jazz. Jackson, who had dropped the "Gator Tail" from his name for Prestige (although he did have a couple of Gator-themed album titles), would be one of their most consistent sellers throughout the 1960s.

McDuff, in turn, would mentor a young guitarist named George Benson, who would go on, in his turn, to become one of the most celebrated jazz guitarists of his generation and then to become one of the most controversial, as his hit records on the pop charts led jazz purists to accuse him, as an earlier generation had accused Nat "King" Cole, of selling out. His response was that if he started and ended with a strong hook, he could play whatever he wanted in the middle—not that different from what could have been said by Jimmy Wright.

The soul jazz decade was the decade of the organ. Richard "Groove" Holmes, Jimmy McGriff, Johnny "Hammond" Smith, and others were prominent. However, the piano was not forgotten, with Horace Silver, Bobby Timmons, and others leaving their mark. Nor were the horns, the traditional lead instruments of jazz. Hank Crawford, who had started with Ray Charles, and Cannonball Adderley, who had started with Miles Davis, became stars of soul jazz.

Conclusion

Two roads diverged in a yellow wood.

—Robert Frost, "The Road Not Taken"

Two roads diverged . . . In 1942, the two roads were Illinois Jacquet and Charlie Parker.

On Central Avenue in Los Angeles, the roads began to diverge even as high school friends Cecil McNeely and William Criss played a Chopin waltz at their graduation. Then, with classmate Hampton Hawes, they formed a jazz group together on that one road through the concrete forest. At the end of Central Avenue, the roads diverged. Up ahead, where they curved and the future was out of view, the travelers were lured by the sounds of two distant horns. Criss and Hawes took the road less traveled, the road of Charlie Parker, which in time would become the main thoroughfare of jazz. Cecil McNeely, now Big Jay, took the road of Illinois Jacquet, which became something all too close to a road to oblivion. But those roads diverged from the same path, didn't they? And that path was swing. That thing that brings all the divergent paths of jazz together. Without which it don't mean a thing.

And maybe they aren't such divergent paths. Maybe Tom Wilson was right, they were "a subtle gradation of . . . important styles which have reached full development since 1940, affecting or being affected by the bop revolution."

That's why Coleman Hawkins was able to play on the first bebop record, why Louis Armstrong could play a duet with Dizzy Gillespie, why Miles Davis could sit in with Jimmy Forrest in a little club in St. Louis, why Oliver Nelson, Jimmy Forrest, and King Curtis could mesh, or Charlie Parker and Machito, why Garvin Bushell could seemingly play with anyone, why Miles could say there's nothing you can play on the trumpet that Armstrong hasn't already played, even the modern stuff.

The musicians who came from the territory bands of the Southwest to Central Avenue, who came to Cincinnati to record for a Black jazzman who had been hired to supervise production for a country and western label, who improvised solos triggered by the bravura singing of a thirteen-year-old boy and his street corner harmonizers, the keyboardists who found new connections between an organ and a tenor saxophone, all found their own way to keep the swing tradition alive.

In 1959 and 1960, the roads diverged again. But if in discussing the rhythm and blues of the 1940s and '50s as jazz, one had to plead the case for R&B's legitimacy, maybe even become defensive at times, this was no longer true. No one had to be vaguely apologetic, in a room full of jazz mavens, for liking Cannonball Adderley, or Jimmy Smith, or Wes Montgomery, or Rahsaan Roland Kirk, or any of the other jazz poll winners who played soul: Charles Mingus (who had started playing with Russell Jacquet and Wynonie Harris on Central Avenue), Milt Jackson, Les McCann, or Horace Silver. Rhythm and blues had finally been subsumed into jazz. In fact, according to *Billboard*, rhythm and blues was no more—in 1963, they discontinued their rhythm and blues and blues chart, saying the music had become so mainstreamed that the chart was no longer needed (they resurrected it in 1965 and then in 1969 changed its name to Soul).

By then, everything was changing. Rock and roll had become rock. It had ceased to be a musical form grounded in rhythm and blues, carried by the wail and honk of a tenor saxophone; it had been turned over mostly to white boys with guitars and had become an international cultural phenomenon. *DownBeat* started covering rock as well as jazz, and *Playboy*'s Jazz Poll became the Jazz and Pop Poll. That new yoking became so ubiquitous that the *Village Voice*'s Robert Christgau started calling his year-end critics' roundup the Pazz and Jop Poll.

Jazz-rock fusion appeared, with rock bands like Chicago adding jazz elements and jazz musicians like Larry Coryell and the Jazz Crusaders adding rock elements. New bands arose, like the Yellowjackets and the Jeff Lorber Fusion, that were created specifically as "fusion" bands. And if there were any questions about the legitimacy of this new genre, they were put to rest when the colossus of contemporary jazz, Miles Davis, announced that he had been listening to Jimi Hendrix, James Brown, and

Sly and the Family Stone, and that he would be incorporating elements of rock into his music—which he did, starting with 1969's *Bitches Brew*.

Today, definitions of jazz are so fluid that an early taxonomist like Leonard Feather would have trouble recognizing it. The closed-caption subtitles of TV movies designate anything that isn't led by guitars or violins as jazz ("ominous jazz," "sprightly jazz," "romantic jazz"). George Benson's recording of "Breezin'" opened the door to something called "smooth jazz," which became popular enough to have its own radio stations and XM or Pandora channels, and its own stars, from Chuck Mangione and Grover Washington to Kenny G. Windham Hill records, in the 1980s and '90s, led by pianist George Winston, offered a musical form that was known as "soft jazz" or "mellow jazz" before it finally settled on "new age music."

These last genres have been denounced by some jazz purists, certainly including those who would champion instrumental rhythm and blues as a legitimate form of jazz, so the jazz culture wars are still going. There are jazz musicians today who consciously reject swing, which one might think to be the sine qua non of jazz.

All music changes. Pianist and educator Billy Taylor has called jazz "America's classical music." What we think of as Europe's classical music changed over the years—a number of times, or perhaps constantly. Jazz changes, redefines itself through the music and is redefined through critical studies. But redefinition is a practice of contemporaneity.

This is certainly not true of political history, where Reconstruction, the Age of Enlightenment, or Athenian democracy are constantly open to revision. But it tends to be true of cultural history, certainly as regards jazz. We know what traditional New Orleans jazz, Chicago style, big band swing, or bebop was. And by those same fixed definitions, we accept that rhythm and blues, although it would appear to have all the characteristics of jazz—improvisation, a connection to the blues, that mysterious quality known as swing—is something separate from jazz. And with all the respect that rhythm and blues has garnered in recent years—as music, as history, as Americana—it has yet to change that definition in the eyes of many who still represent the jazz establishment.

But to others, listening to the music played along all those highways and byways—the road less traveled, the road more traveled, the road of vagabonds and the road of commercial travelers—they can be appreciated as all the same road, the one that has its name up on the signpost at 52nd Street and 6th Avenue: Swing Street.

Acknowledgments

I owe this book to a lot of people, starting with two sets of brothers who ventured into adolescence at the dawn of the rock and roll era: Tad and Jon Richards, Peter and Wendy Jones, who discovered this new music and embraced it fervently, buying 78 RPM records and then the new 45s, finding out that the music which spoke to us most deeply was not that of the white teen idols like Paul Anka and Frankie Avalon, but the music that came from a deeper source, that spoke to us from a place that was beyond our experience, but that we needed to hear about. We started together on a journey that was to end much too young for Wendy, who shared my passion most deeply, but Jon and Peter have stayed with me for a long and satisfying lifetime, listening with me, listening to me, encouraging me to believe that this is important.

I owe it to writers and editors and musicians along the way who have helped and encouraged me. So many. I'll mention a few who are gone. Heywood Hale Broun, who went on a journey of his own, seeking out and recording the forgotten musicians of New Orleans in 1940 and sparking a New Orleans jazz revival. Richard Daniel and Tim Ingles, who didn't seem to notice, or care much, that I was white, and seemed to think I could write songs that they wanted to play. Bob Abel, my first editor, who taught me so much about what should go into and what should be left out of a book.

And I owe it people who know more than I'll ever know about music and who I could turn to for help and encouragement. Thanks, Larry "the Fluff" Audette. Thanks, T. Brooks Shepard. Thanks to Morris Holbrook, who read so much of this manuscript and helped so much with his feedback. Thanks to Billy Vera, for stories I could have gotten nowhere else, and Dan Tomassi, Jimmy Wright's son. And many others. Thanks to musicians like Eric Parker, John Hall, Pete Levin, and others, for helping me out on the difference between swing and shuffle, and other questions.

I owe it to my daughters—Charis, Caitlin, and Wendy—for love and support and not thinking I was too crazy. And gratitude to Caitlin for telling me she was thankful for growing up in a house where so many different kinds of music were played.

I owe it to my wife, Pat, for believing in me and keeping our lives together in all the ways I'm hopeless at.

And I very much owe it to my editor, Richard Carlin, for recognizing that this music belongs in the story of jazz and deserves a book of its own on the jazz shelf. And for making it better.

And to so many more in my life who've encouraged my passions. And all the names that I'll kick myself for not remembering to put in until it was too late. Thanks to all of you.

Notes

Notes to the Introduction

1. In the 1956 movie *The Benny Goodman Story*, Benny, played by Steve Allen, voices his dissatisfaction with "sweet" music and his desire to play "hot" music. The word "jazz" is never uttered by any character.

Notes to Chapter 1

1. Discographical information on old 78 RPM records is extremely difficult to find. For this and most of the other discographies of old 78s, I have relied on 45worlds.com.

2. JazzTimesVideos. "Saxophonist James Carter on Illinois Jacquet and More." YouTube, March 24, 2016, https://www.youtube.com/watch?v=NDwFJgpX6M M&t=151s, accessed October 17, 2022.

3. Stephen Koch, *Louis Jordan Son of Arkansas, Father of R&B*, History Press, 2014.

4. Almost all of these recordings can be listened to online. Most of them are on YouTube, on the various streaming services, or on websites devoted to old blues and jazz.

5. A highly regarded contemporary rock and R&B drummer (Ian Hunter Band, John Hall Band), Parker is one of five drumming brothers and the son of jazz drummer Robert Parker.

6. Jordan starred in the musical comedies *Beware* (1946) and *Reet Petite and Gone* (1947), and appeared in *Miss Bobby Socks* (1944), *Follow the Boys* (1944), *Swingtime Jamboree* (1946), and *Swing Parade of 1946*, as well as making "soundies" (short musical films that were not affected by the Petrillo ban).

Notes to Chapter 2

1. This was not Eddie "Lockjaw" Davis, a lifelong New Yorker. But McNeely's memory shows the breadth of jazz careers for the young men who grew up together in Watts and South Central. Reed man Buddy Collette, a musician of great versatility, formed a small-group swing ensemble in 1946 with his close friend Charles Mingus. Called the Stars of Swing, it also featured Britt Woodman, Lucky Thompson, and Teddy Edwards (and it's a shame they never recorded). Collette is perhaps best known for his work with Chico Hamilton in the cool West Coast style; his other associations ranged from Joe Liggins to Groucho Marx (who fought racism to hire him as the only Black member of the *You Bet Your Life* studio orchestra). As a teacher, his students included Eric Dolphy and Charles Lloyd.

Of the five talented Woodman brothers, trombonist Britt made the biggest mark in jazz. Best known for his work with Duke Ellington, he also played soul jazz with Jimmy Smith and avant garde jazz with John Coltrane. He worked frequently with his old friend Charles Mingus.

Walter Benton recorded with Clifford Brown and Max Roach, Quincy Jones, and Victor Feldman, among others. Walter Henry recorded with James Von Streeter and Johnny Otis, as well as cutting some sides with his own band for Imperial Records. Clifford Solomon's rhythm and blues band that cut some sides for Okeh included Max Roach, Jimmy Cleveland, and Monk Montgomery, with a vocal by Gigi Gryce. He also recorded with Gryce, Art Farmer, and Lionel Hampton.

2. New York's cabaret laws prohibited dancing in small clubs, so bebop with its tricky rhythms and extended virtuoso solos became known as music for listening, not dancing. But in LA, and in jazz outposts like Detroit, people danced to their favorite modernists and to visiting stars. One Detroit club even had Charlie Parker playing to a line of chorus girls.

3. McNeely's reminiscence is included in *Central Avenue Sounds*, a collection of oral histories edited by a team led by Clora Bryant.

Notes to Chapter 3

1. This would actually contribute to the demise of their record labels in the early 1950s, when 45 RPM records came along, and they were only set up to press 78s.

Notes to Chapter 4

1. Some of the other musicians on the session were Dizzy Gillespie, Marvin Stamm, Jon Faddis, Zoot Sims, Joe Farrell, Seldon Powell, David "Fathead" Newman, Gerry Mulligan, Herbie Mann, James Booker, and Warren Bernhardt.

2. Quoted in Sally Brockman, "Nellie Lutcher's Musical Journey," *Visit Lake Charles*, October 8, 2019, https://www.visitlakecharles.org/blog/post/about-nellie-lutcher/.

3. Late in his career, Prysock did play standards, successfully touring to accompany his brother Arthur, a ballad singer in the Johnny Hartman/Billy Eckstine mode.

4. Atlantic never released it, and it eventually turned up on a Swedish label.

Notes to Chapter 6

1. What exists of this interview is a very poor written transcript, with most of the names impossibly mangled, so I've cleaned it up for purposes of clarity.

2. From a text conversation with Peter Jones, 2022.

3. All the quotes from Vera come from interviews conducted by text over a period of a few weeks in 2022.

Notes to Chapter 8

1. Prestige also signed up Hal "Cornbread" Singer, but he didn't have the success that Jackson had.

Works Cited

Abbott, Jim. "Saxophone Great Noble 'Thin Man' Watts Dies." *Orlando Sentinel*, August 26, 2004.

Brockman, Sally. "Nellie Lutcher's Musical Journey." *Visit Lake Charles*, October 8, 2019, https://www.visitlakecharles.org/blog/post/about-nellie-lutcher/.

Broven, John. *Rhythm and Blues in New Orleans*. Pelican Publishing Company, 2016.

Bryant, Clora, and Steven Louis Isoardi. *Central Avenue Sounds*. Regents of the University of California, 1994.

Charters, Samuel B., and Leonard Kunstadt. *Jazz: A History of the New York Scene*. Da Capo Press, 1984.

Dawson, Jim. *Nervous Man Nervous: Big Jay McNeely and the Rise of the Honking Tenor Sax!* Big Nickel Publications, 1994.

Earl Bostic, https://earlbostic.com/.

Eastman, Ralph. "Central Avenue Blues: The Making of Los Angeles Rhythm and Blues, 1942–1947." *Black Music Research Journal*, 1989.

Feather, Leonard. *The Encyclopedia of Jazz*. Da Capo Press, 1960.

Gendron, Bernard. "Moldy Figs and Modernists: Jazz at War (1942–1946)." *Discourse*, 1993.

George, Nelson. *The Death of Rhythm and Blues*. Penguin Books, 2004.

Gitler, Ira. *Swing to Bop*. Oxford University Press, 1985.

Goldberg, Joe. *Jazz Masters of the Fifties*. Da Capo Press, 1983.

Griffith, Mark. "Earl Palmer Remembered." *Modern Drummer Magazine*, https://www.moderndrummer.com/2009/01/earl-palmer/.

Hannusch, Jeff. *I Hear You Knockin': The Sound of New Orleans Rhythm and Blues*. Swallow Publications, 1989.

Hannusch, Jeff. *The Soul of New Orleans: A Legacy of Rhythm and Blues*. Swallow Publications, 2001.

Hogan Jazz Archives, Interview with Alvin "Red" Tyler, https://musicrising.tulane.edu/listen/interviews/alvin-red-tyler-1996-06-19/.

"Interview with Dave Bartholomew [Part 1 of 2]." *GBH Openvault*, https://openvault.wgbh.org/catalog/V_C62E90C1D5B74587AD6FBFF0A83A7107.

"Interview with Dave Bartholomew [Part 2 of 2]." *GBH Openvault*, https://open vault.wgbh.org/catalog/V_7BF6300CAD044620ACCFFE0A8D4E52EA.

JazzTimesVideos. "Saxophonist James Carter on Illinois Jacquet and More." YouTube, March 24, 2016, https://www.youtube.com/watch?v=NDwFJgpX6MM &t=151s.

Kerouac, Jack. *On the Road*. Penguin Classics, 2022.

Koch, Stephen. *Louis Jordan Son of Arkansas, Father of R&B*. History Press, 2014.

Lillard, Dick. "Joe Liggins and Roy Milton." *Blues and Rhythm*, June 2021, pp. 16–17.

Marmorstein, Gary. "Central Avenue Jazz: Los Angeles Black Music of the Forties." *Southern California Quarterly*, 1988, pp. 415–426.

McCord, Jeff. "The State of Illinois." *Texas Monthly*, November 1, 2002, https://www.texasmonthly.com/articles/the-state-of-illinois/.

Morgan, Thomas. "Tracing the Rich Heritage of Rhythm and Blues." *New York Times*, February 10, 1986.

Myers, Marc. "Interview: Big Jay McNeely (Part 1)." *JazzWax*, https://www.jazzwax.com/2009/07/interview-big-jay-mcneely-part-1.html.

Myers, Marc. "Interview: Big Jay McNeely (Part 2)." *JazzWax*, https://www.jazzwax.com/2009/07/interview-big-jay-mcneely-part-2.html.

"One Hit Wonders: Sil Austin." *One Hit Wonders*, http://www.onehitwondersthe-book.com/?page_id=1684.

Otis, Johnny. "Roy Milton Interview." *Blues and Rhythm*, June 2021.

Otis, Johnny. *Upside Your Head!: Rhythm and Blues on Central Avenue*. Wesleyan University Press, 2010.

Porter, Bob. *Soul Jazz: Jazz in the Black Community, 1945–1975*. Xlibris, 2016.

Propes, Steve. "Joe Liggins, a Honey of an R&B Man." *Los Angeles Times*, August 19, 1987.

Shaw, Arnold. *Honkers and Shouters: The Golden Years of Rhythm and Blues*. Collier Books/Macmillan, 1978.

Tomkins, Les. "Illinois Jacquet." *National Jazz Archive*, March 27, 2020, https://nationaljazzarchive.org.uk/explore/interviews/1633367-illinois-jacquet.

Townsend, Peter. *Pearl Harbor Jazz: Change in Popular Music in the Early 1940s*. University Press of Mississippi, 2007.

Ulanov, Barry. *A Handbook of Jazz*. Greenwood, 1975.

Ward, Brian. *Just My Soul Responding: Rhythm and Blues, Black Consciousness, and Race Relations*. Routledge, 2004.

Wexler, Jerry. *Rhythm and the Blues*. St. Martin's Press, 1994.

Whitburn, Joel. *Joel Whitburn Presents Hot R & B Songs, 1942–2010*. Record Research Inc., 2010.

Discography

Artists Discussed in This Book

This discography is for those who want to hear more of this music and lists recordings that can be purchased on CD or vinyl or streamed on the popular streaming services.

Allen, Lee. *Walkin' with Mr. Lee.* Collectables.
Atlantic Rhythm and Blues 1947–1974. 8-CD box set. Atlantic.
Austin, Sil. *Swingsation.* Polygram Records.
Austin, Sil, and Red Prysock. *Battle Royal.* Mercury.
Bagby, Doc. *Smooth Organ, Groove Organ: Includes The Complete Honky Tonk in Silk Plus over 20 of His Hottest Organ 45s of the 1950s.* Jasmine Music.
Bartholomew, Dave. *Jump Children!: The Imperial Singles Plus 1950–1962.* Jasmine Music
Bartholomew, Dave. *The Big Beat of Dave Bartholomew: 20 of His Milestone New Orleans Productions 1949–1960.* Bartholomew as producer/bandleader. Recordings by Fats Domino, Smiley Lewis, Archibald, Shirley and Lee, etc. Capitol.
Big Maybelle. *The Very Best of Big Maybelle.* Notnow.
Bostic, Earl. *His Finest Albums.* 4-CD box set. Enlightenment.
Bradshaw, Tiny. *The Very Best of Tiny Bradshaw.* Collectables.
Brown, Charles. *The Cool Cool Blues of . . . Charles Brown: All-Time Classic Hits and R&B Chart Hits 1945–1961.* Jasmine Music.
Brown, Ruth. *The Queen of R&B: The Singles & Albums Collection 1949–61.* Acrobat.
Charles, Ray. *Genius + Soul = Jazz.* Impulse!
Charles, Ray. *Rock and Roll.* Atlantic.
Cole, Nat "King." *Early 1940s.* Mark56 Records.
Culley, Frank "Floorshow," and Buddy Tate, *Rock and Roll Instrumentals for Dancing the Lindy Hop.* LP only. Baton.
Curtis, King. *The New Scene of King Curtis + Soul Meeting.* Aim Records.

Curtis, King. *Instant Soul: The Legendary King Curtis.* Razor & Tie.

Davis, Eddie "Lockjaw," and Shirley Scott. *Jazz with a Beat.* King.

Davis, Eddie "Lockjaw," and Shirley Scott. *Eddie "Lockjaw" Davis Cookbook.* Prestige.

Davis, Wild Bill. *Collection 1951–60.* Acrobat.

Ding Dong / Gee Records Story. Tenor sax solos by Jimmy Wright and one Wright instrumental. 2-CD box set. One Day Music.

Doggett, Bill. *Dancing with Bill Doggett, His Organ and Combo 1955–1960.* Jasmine Music.

Forrest, Jimmy. *Night Train.* Delmark.

Forrest, Jimmy, and Miles Davis. *Our Delight: Recorded Live at the Barrel, St. Louis.* Prestige.

Freed, Alan, Rock 'n' Roll Big Band. *A Stompin' Good Time.* Featuring King Curtis, Sam "the Man" Taylor, Al Sears, Kenny Burrell, others. Ace Records UK.

Gant, Cecil. *Collection 1944–51.* 2-CD box set. Acrobat.

Gaillard, Slim. *Slim's Jam.* Drive Archive.

Gayten, Paul. *True (You Don't Love Me): Early Recordings 1947–1949.* Jasmine Music.

Grimes, Tiny. *1951–54.* Classics.

Hardesty, Herb. *Domino Effect: Wing & Federal Recordings 1958–1961.* Ace Records UK.

Harris, Wynonie. *Blow Your Brains Out: Greatest Jukebox Hits & Dancefloor Favourites.* Jasmine Music.

Howard, Camille. *X-Temporaneous Boogie.* Specialty.

Jackson, Bull Moose. *I Want a Bowlegged Woman: The Greatest Hits 1945–1955.* Jasmine Music.

Jackson, Willis. *A One-Day Session 05/25/59 with Jack McDuff & Bill Jennings.* FS World Jazz.

Jackson, Willis. *Doin' the Gator Tail: Tenor Sax Blasting 1949–1959.* Jasmine Music.

Jacquet, Illinois. *Collection: 1942–1956.* 2-CD box set. Includes "Flying Home" with Lionel Hampton and "Blues Pt. 2" with Jazz at the Philharmonic. Acrobat.

Johnson, Buddy. *Rock On! The 100th Anniversary Collection: Twenty Years of Blues, Boogie and Ballads 1941–1961.* Jasmine Music.

Johnson, Plas. *The Best of Plas Johnson.* Wolf Records.

Jordan, Louis. *Louis Jordan and His Tympany Five.* 5-CD box set. Jsp Records.

King R&B. 4-CD box set. Includes Wynonie Harris, Roy Brown, Tiny Bradshaw, Bill Doggett, Earl Bostic, others. Gusto.

Liggins, Joe. *Collection: 1944–57.* 3-CD box set. Acrobat.

Lucas, Buddy. *Rockin', Boppin' & Hoppin' 1951–1962.* Jasmine Music.

Lutcher, Nellie. *The Best of Nellie Lutcher.* Capitol Jazz.

Lymon, Frankie. *The Very Best of Frankie Lymon & the Teenagers.* Jimmy Wright tenor sax solos. Flashback-Rhino.

McDuff, Brother Jack. *The Honeydripper.* Prestige.

McNeely, Big Jay. *King of the Honkers: Selected Singles 1948–1952.* Jasmine Music.

McShann, Jay. *1941–43*. Includes Charlie Parker solos on "Hootie Blues" and "Sepian Bounce." Classics.

McVea, Jack. *McVoutie's Central Avenue Blues*. Does not include "Open the Door, Richard." Delmark.

Millinder, Lucky. *Are You Ready to Rock: Singles 1942–1955*. Jasmine Music.

Milton, Roy. *Collection: 1945–61*. 2-CD box set. Acrobat.

Moore, Johnny, Three Blazers. *Singles Collection 1945–52*. 3-CD Box Set. Acrobat.

Moore, Wild Bill. *Complete Volume 2: 1948–1955*. Blue Moon Imports.

Morris, Joe. *Anytime, Anyplace, Anywhere*. Acrobat.

Nelson, Oliver, with Jimmy Forrest and King Curtis. *Soul Battle*. Prestige.

Newman, David "Fathead." *Fathead: Ray Charles Presents David Newman*. Rhino Wea UK.

Otis, Johnny. *The Johnny Otis Rhythm & Blues Caravan: The Complete Savoy Recordings*. 3-CD box set. Savoy Jazz.

Palmer, Earl. *Backbeat: The World's Greatest Drummer, Ever!* Palmer on recordings by Little Richard, Lee Allen, Charles Brown, Etta James, Fats Domino, etc. Ace Records UK.

Prysock, Red. *Best of Red Prysock*. Avi Entertainment.

Regal Records in New Orleans. Paul Gayten, Annie Laurie, Dave Bartholomew, Roy Brown. Specialty.

Singer, Hal. *Rent Party*. Savoy Jazz.

Smith, Jimmy. *Best of Jimmy Smith the Blue Note Years*. Blue Note.

Specialty Story. 5-CD box set. Includes recordings by Roy Milton, Camille Howard, Joe Lutcher, Jimmy Liggins, Joe Liggins, Little Richard, others. Specialty.

Taylor, Sam "the Man." *Swingsation*. Verve.

Tyler, Alvin "Red." *Heritage*. Rounder.

Vinson, Eddie "Cleanhead." *Mr. Cleanhead Blows His Greatest Hits: Selected Singles 1944–1950*. Jasmine Music.

Walker, T-Bone. *Ultimate Collection 1929–57*. 5-CD box set. Acrobat.

Watts, Noble "Thin Man." *Honkin', Shakin' & Slidin': A Singles Collection 1954–1962*. Jasmine Music.

Williams, Paul. *Doin' The Hucklebuck & Other Jukebox Favourites 1948–1955*. Jasmine Music.

Historical Discography

The records referred to in this book, in order of appearance in the text.

CHAPTER ONE: JACQUET AND JORDAN

Jay McShann and His Orchestra, "Lonely Boy Blues" (McShann, Brown) / "Sepian Bounce" (McShann). Orville Minor, Buddy Anderson, Bob Merrill (tp)

Lawrence Anderson, Taswell Baird (tb), John Jackson, Charlie Parker (as), Fred Culliver, Bob Mabane (ts), James Coe (bar), Jay McShann (p), Leonard "Lucky" Enois (g), Gene Ramey (b), Gus Johnson (d), Walter Brown, Al Hibbler (vcl), Skip Hall, William J. Scott (arr). New York, July 2, 1942. Decca 4387, 78 RPM record.

Lionel Hampton and His Orchestra, "Flying Home" (Goodman, Hampton) / "In the Bag" (Hampton, Crowder). Eddie "Gogo" Hutchinson, Manny Klein, Ernie Royal, Jack Trainor (tp), Fred Beckett, Sonny Craven, Harry Sloan (tb), Marshal Royal (cl, as), Ray Perry (as, vln), Eddie Barefield, Illinois Jacquet (ts), Jack McVea (bar), Lionel Hampton (vib, arr), Milt Buckner (p), Irving Ashby (g), Vernon Alley (b), Lee Young (d), Rubel Blakey (vcl). New York, May 26, 1942. Decca 18394, 78 RPM record.

Louis Jordan and His Tympany Five, "I'm Gonna Leave You on the Outskirts of Town" (Jordan, Weldon) / "It's a Low Down Dirty Shame" (Shepard). Eddie Roane (tp, backing vcl), Louis Jordan (as, ts, vcl), Arnold Thomas (p), Dallas Bartley (b), Walter Martin (d). New York, July 21, 1942. Decca 8638, 78 RPM record.

Louis Jordan and His Tympany Five, "The Chicks I Pick Are Slender and Tender and Tall" (Jackson) / "What's the Use of Getting Sober (When You're Gonna Get Drunk Again)" (Meyers). Personnel and recording date same as above. Decca 23629, 78 RPM record.

Jay McShann and His Orchestra, "Confessin' the Blues" (McShann/Brown) / "Hootie Blues" (Parker/McShann). Harold Bruce, Buddy Anderson, Orville Minor (tp), Taswell Baird (tb), John Jackson (as), Charlie Parker (as, arr), Harold Ferguson, Bob Mabane (ts), Jay McShann (p), Gene Ramey (b), Gus Johnson (d), Walter Brown (vcl), William J. Scott (arr). Dallas, April 30, 1941. Decca 8559, 78 RPM record.

Norman Granz' Jazz at the Philharmonic, "Blues, Part 1" / "Blues, Part 2" (by the Ensemble). J. J. Johnson (tb), Illinois Jacquet, Jack McVea (ts), Nat King Cole (p), Les Paul (g), Johnny Miller (b), Lee Young (d). Los Angeles, July 2, 1946. Disc 6024, 78 RPM record.

Illinois Jacquet, "Flying Home Part 1" / "Flying Home Part 2" (Goodman/Hampton). Russell Jacquet (tp, vcl), Henry Coker (tb), Illinois Jacquet (ts), Arthur Dennis (bar), Sir Charles Thompson (p), Ulysses Livingston (g), Billy Hadnott (b), Johnny Otis (d). Los Angeles, July, 1945. Aladdin Jazz Series 101, 78 RPM record.

Illinois Jacquet and His All Stars, "Memories of You" (Blake/Razaf) / "Merle's Mood" (Jacquet). Russell Jacquet (tp, vcl), John Brown (as), Illinois Jacquet (ts), Arthur Dennis (bar), Bill Doggett (p), Ulysses Livingston (g), Charles Mingus (b), Al "Cake" Wichard (d). Hollywood, August 2, 1945. Apollo 760, 78 RPM record.

Illinois Jacquet, "Ghost of a Chance" (Crosby-Washington-Young) / "Bottoms Up" (Jacquet), Same personnel and date. Apollo 756, 78 RPM record.

Chick Webb's Savoy Orchestra, "I Can't Dance (I've Got Ants in My Pants)" (Williams, Gaines) / "Imagination" (Van Heusen). Mario Bauza, Reunald Jones (tp), Taft Jordan (tp, vcl), Sandy Williams (tb), Pete Clarke (cl, as), Edgar Sampson (as, arr), Elmer Williams (cl, ts), Joe Steele (p), John Trueheart (bj, g), John Kirby (b), Chick Webb (d), Chuck Richards, Louis Jordan (vcl). New York, May 9, 1934. Columbia 2920. 78 RPM record.

Rodney Sturgis with Lovie Jordon's Elks Rendezvous Band (Louis Jordan), "Toodle Loo on Down" (Williams-Sturgis) / "The Gal That Wrecked My Life" (Sturgis). Rodney Sturgis (vcl) acc by Courtney Williams (tp), Louis Jordan (as, ts, bar), Lem Johnson (ts), Clarence Johnson (p), Charlie Drayton (b), Walter Martin (d). New York, December 20, 1938. Decca 7550, 78 RPM record.

Rodney Sturgis with Louie Jordon's Elks Rendezvous Band (Louis Jordan), "So Good" / "Away from You" (Sturgis). Same date, personnel. Decca 7579, 78 RPM record.

Louis Jordan and His Tympany Five, "Honeysuckle Rose" (Waller-Razaf) / "But I'll Be Back" (Jordan). Courtney Williams (tp), Louis Jordan (as, bar), Stafford "Pazzuza" Simon (fl, cl, ts), Clarence Johnson (p), Charlie Drayton (b), Walter Martin (d). New York, November 14, 1939. Decca 7675, 78 RPM record.

Louie Jordan and His Tympany Five, "Flat Face" (Williams) / "Doug the Jitterbug" (Jordan). Courtney Williams (tp), Louis Jordan (as, ts, bar, voc), Lem Johnson (ts), Clarence Johnson (p), Charlie Drayton (b), Walter Martin (d, tymp). New York, March 29, 1939. Decca 7590, 78 RPM.

Louis Jordan and His Tympany Five "That'll Just About Knock Me Out" (Williams-Wilson) / "Five Guys Named Moe" (Bresler-Wynn). Eddie Roane (tp, backing vcl), Louis Jordan (as, ts, vcl), Arnold Thomas (p), Dallas Bartley (b), Walter Martin (d). July 21, 1942. Decca 8653, 78 RPM record.

Louis Jordan and His Tympany Five, "Saturday Night Fish Fry (Part 1)" / "Saturday Night Fish Fry (Conclusion)" (Jordan-Walsh). Aaron Izenhall, Bob Mitchell, Harold Mitchell (tp), Louis Jordan (as, vcl), Josh Jackson (ts), Bill Doggett (p, arr), Ham Jackson (el-g), Billy Hadnott (b), Christopher Columbus (d) [as Joe Morris (d)]. Decca 24725, 78 RPM record.

Louis Jordan and His Tympany Five, "Beware" (Lasco-Moore-Adams) / "Don't Let the Sun Catch You Cryin'" (Greene). Aaron Izenhall (tp), Louis Jordan (as, vcl), Josh Jackson (ts), Wild Bill Davis (p, arr), Carl Hogan (el-g), Jesse "Po" Simpkins (b), Eddie Byrd (d). August 9, 1949. Decca 18818, 78 RPM record.

Louis Jordan and His Tympany Five, "Ration Blues" (Jordan-Casey-Clark) / "Deacon Jones" (Lange-Heath-Loring). Eddie Roane (tp), Louis Jordan (as, ts-1, vcl), Arnold Thomas (p), Jesse "Po" Simpkins (b), Shadow Wilson (d), Duke of Iron, Sister Rosetta Tharpe (vcl). October 4, 1943. Decca 8654, 78 RPM record.

Louis Jordan and His Tympany Five, "G. I. Jive" (Mercer) / "Is You Is or Is You Ain't (Ma Baby)" (Austin-Jordan). Eddie Roane (tp), Louis Jordan (as, ts-1, vcl), Arnold Thomas (p), Jesse "Po" Simpkins, Al Morgan (b), Shadow Wilson, Slick Jones (d), Duke of Iron, Sister Rosetta Tharpe (vcl). New York, October 4, 1943, March 15, 1944. Decca 8659, 78 RPM record.

CHAPTER TWO: THE WAR YEARS: LOS ANGELES'S CENTRAL AVENUE

The Johnny Otis Show, "Willie and the Hand Jive" / "Ring-a-Ling." Personnel unidentified. April 3, 1958. Capitol Records 3966, 45 RPM record.

Les Hite and His Orchestra, vocal by T-Bone Walker, "T-Bone Blues" (Walker-Hite) / "It Must Have Been a Dream" (Hite). Paul Campbell, Walter Williams, Forrest Powell (tp), Britt Woodman, Allen Durham (tb), Les Hite (as), Floyd Turnham (cl, as), Que Martyn, Roger Hurd (cl, ts), Sol Moore (bar), Nat Walker (p), Frank Pasley (g), Al Morgan (b), Oscar Lee Bradley, Jr. (d), T-Bone Walker (vcl), Dudley Brooks (arr). Los Angeles, June 1940. Varsity 8391, 78 RPM record.

Freddie Slack and his Orchestra, "He's My Guy" (DePaul, Raye) / "Doll Dance" (Brown). Personnel for "He's My Guy" only: George Wendt, Don Anderson, Clyde Hurley (tp), Bill Anthens, Ed Kusby (tb), Blake Reynolds (as, cl), Bumps Myers (ts), Art Smith, Al Taylor (reeds), Freddie Slack (p), T-Bone Walker (g), Fred Whiting (b), Rich Cornell (d), Ella Mae Morse, Johnny Mercer (vcl), Gaye Jones (arr). Los Angeles, July 20, 1942. Capitol 113, 78 RPM record.

Joe Liggins and his Honeydrippers, "The Honeydripper Part 1" / "The Honey-dripper Part 2" (Liggins). Joe Liggins (vcl, p) acc by Little Willie Jackson (as, bar), James Jackson (ts), Frank Pasley (g), Red Callender (b), Peppy Prince (d). Los Angeles, March 26, 1945. Exclusive 207, 78 RPM record.

Herb Jeffries With Joe Liggins' Honeydrippers, "Left a Good Deal in Mobile" (Jeffries-Leslie) / "Here's Hoping" (Rene). Herb Jeffries (vcl) acc by Little Willie Jackson (as, bar), James Jackson (ts), Joe Liggins (p), Frank Pasley (g), Eddy Davis (b), Peppy Prince (d). Los Angeles, 1945. Exclusive 208, 78 RPM record.

Joe Liggins and His Honeydrippers, "Blue Moods" (Liggins) / "I've Got a Right to Cry" (Liggins). Joe Liggins (vcl, p) acc by Little Willie Jackson (as, bar, sop), James Jackson (ts), Frank Pasley (g), Red Callender (b), Peppy Prince (d). Side B add Joe Darensbourg (cl). Los Angeles, March 28, April 20, 1945. Exclusive 210, 78 RPM record.

CHAPTER THREE: A NEW SOUND

Lucky Millinder and His Orchestra, "Who Threw the Whiskey in the Well" (DeLange-Brooks) / "Shipyard Social Function" (Millinder-Smith). Infor-mation for "Whiskey" only: Freddie Webster, Ludwig "Joe" Jordan, Curtis Murphy, Leroy Elton Hill (tp); Gene Simon, Al Cobbs, Joe Britton (tb);

Preston Love, Bill Swindell (as); Elmer Williams, Eddie "Lockjaw" Davis
(ts); Lucky Thompson (ts-1); Ernest Leavey (bar); Ellis Larkins (p); Lawrence "Larry" Lucie (g); Al McKibbon (b); Panama Francis (d); Wynonie
Harris, ensemble (vcl); Lucky Millinder (ldr). New York, May 25, 1944.
Decca 18674, 78 RPM record.

Wynonie "Mr. Blues" Harris with Johnny Otis' All Stars, "Around the Clock Blues,
Parts 1 and 2" (Harris). Wynonie Harris (vcl) acc by: Howard McGhee
(tp-1), Teddy Edwards (ts), Lee Wesley Jones (p), Stanley Morgan (g), Bob
Kesterson (b), Johnny Otis (d). Los Angeles, June–July 1945. Philo/Aladdin
103, 78 RPM record.

Wynonie "Mr. Blues" Harris with Johnny Otis' All Stars, "Cock-a-Doodle Doo"
(Harris) / "Yonder Goes My Baby" (Harris). Same personnel and date.
Philo/Aladdin 104, 78 RPM record.

Wynonie Harris with the Hamp-Tone All Stars, "Hey-ba-ba-re-bop, Parts 1 and
2" (Hammer-Hampton). Wynonie Harris (vcl) acc by Joe Morris, Wendell
Culley (tp), Herbie Fields (cl, ts), Arnett Cobb (ts), Charlie Fowlkes (bar),
Milt Buckner (p), Billy Mackel (g), Charlie Harris (b), George Jenkins (d).
Los Angeles, September 1945. Hamp-tone HT-100, 78 RPM record.

Wynonie "Mr. Blues" Harris, "Dig This Boogie" (Harris) / "Lightnin' Struck the
Poor House" (Harris). Wynonie Harris (vcl) acc by Jackie Allen (tp), Jimmie
Jackson (as), Herman "Sonny" Blount (aka Sun Ra) (p), poss. Wynonie
Harris (d). Nashville, May 14, 1946. Bullet 251, 78 RPM record.

Wynonie Harris, "Good Rockin' Tonight" (Brown) / "Good Morning Mr. Blues"
(Harris). Wynonie Harris (vcl) acc by: Hot Lips Page (tp), Joe Britton (tb),
Vincent Bair-Bey (as), Hal Singer, Tom Archia (ts), Earl Knight (p), Carl
"Flat Top" Wilson (b), Bobby Donaldson (d). Cincinnati, December 28,
1947. King 4210, 79 RPM record.

Big Maybelle with Tiny Bradshaw Orchestra, "Indian Giver" (Jacobs-Blackman) /
"Too Tight Mama" (Blackman). Big Maybelle (as Mabel Smith) (vcl), acc by
Hot Lips Page (tp), Joe Britton (tb-2), Vincent Bair-Bey (as-2), Hal Singer,
Tom Archia (ts), Earl Knight (p), Lonnie Johnson (el-g), Carl "Flat-Top"
Wilson (b), Bobby Donaldson (d). Cincinnati, November or early December
1947 and December 23, 1947. King 4227, 78 RPM record.

Big Maybelle with Tiny Bradshaw Orchestra, "Bad Dream Blues" (Blackman,
Smith) / "Sad and Disappointed Jill" (Blackman). Same personnel. Cincinnati, November or early December 1947 and December 28, 1947. King
4207, 78 RPM record.

Marion Abernathy with Tiny Bradshaw Orchestra, "My Man Boogie" / "Wee
Baby." Marion Abernathy (vcl) acc by Hot Lips Page (tp), Joe Britton (tb),
Hal Singer, Tom Archia (ts), Vincent Bair-bey (as, bar), Earl Knight (p),
Carl "Flat Top" Wilson (b), Bobby Donaldson (d). Cincinnati, December
23, December 28, 1947. Federal 12028, 78 RPM record.

Roy Milton and his Solid Senders, "R. M. Blues" (Milton) / "Rhythm Cocktail" (Milton). Hosea Sapp (tp), Earl Sims (as), Buddy Floyd (ts), Camille Howard (p, vcl), Dave Robinson (b), Roy Milton (d, vcl-1). Hollywood, December 22, 1945. Jukebox JB504, Specialty 504, 78 RPM record.

Camille Howard Trio, "You Don't Love Me" (Albert) / "X-Temporaneous Boogie" (Howard). Camille Howard (p), Johnny Rogers (g), Dallas Bartley (b), Roy Milton (d). Los Angeles, December 31, 1947. Specialty 307, 78 RPM record.

Chapter Four: Postwar Explosion

Pvt. Cecil Gant, "I Wonder" (Gant) / "Cecil Boogie" (Gant). Cecil Gant (p, vcl), other personnel unknown. Los Angeles, 1944, release date September 1944. Gilt-Edge 501, 78 RPM record.

Johnny Moore's Three Blazers, "Drifting Blues" (Three Blazers) / "Groovy" (Three Blazers). Charles Brown (vcl, p), Johnny Moore (g), Eddie Williams (b), Johnny Otis (d). Los Angeles, September 11, 1945. Aladdin 112, 78 RPM record.

Charles Brown, "Please Come Home for Christmas" (Brown-Redd) / "Christmas Comes But Once a Year" (Milburn). Charles Brown (p, vcl), other personnel unknown. Release date 1960. King 5405, 45 RPM record.

Nellie Lutcher and Her Rhythm, "Hurry on Down" (Lutcher) / "The Lady's in Love with You" (Lane, Loesser). Nellie Lutcher (p, vcl) Ulysses Livingston (g), Billy Hadnott (b), Lee Young (d). Los Angeles, April 10, 1947. Capitol 40002, 78 RPM record.

Nellie Lutcher and Her Rhythm, "He's a Real Gone Guy" (Lutcher) / "Let Me Love You Tonight" (Parrish, Touzet). Nellie Lutcher (p, vcl), Nappy Lamare (g), Billy Hadnott (b), Lee Young (d). Los Angeles, April 20, 1947. Capitol 400017, 78 RPM record.

Nellie Lutcher and Her Rhythm, "Sleepy Lagoon" (Coates, Lawrence) / "The Song Is Ended" (Berlin). Nellie Lutcher (p, vcl), Irving Ashby (g), Billy Hadnott (b), Sidney Catlett (d). Los Angeles, August 26, 1947. Capitol 10109, 78 RPM record.

Nellie Lutcher and Her Rhythm, "Fine Brown Frame" (Cartiero-Williams) / "The Pig-Latin Song" (Lutcher). (A) Nellie Lutcher (p, vcl), Hurley Ramey (g), Truck Parham (b), Alvin Burroughs (d). Chicago, December 27, 1947. (B) Nellie Lutcher (p, vcl), Ulysses Livingston (g), Billy Hadnott (b), Lee Young (d). Los Angeles, August 17, 1947. Capitol 15032, 78 RPM record.

Nat King Cole and Nellie Lutcher, "For You My Love" (Gayten) / "Can I Come in for a Second?" (Cahn). Nat King Cole (vcl, p), acc by Ernie Royal (tp), Charlie Barnet (ts), Irving Ashby (g), Joe Comfort (b), Earl Hyde (d), Nellie Lutcher (vcl). Los Angeles, January 5, 1950. Capitol 847, 78 RPM record.

Tiny Bradshaw and His Orchestra, "These Things Are Love' (Bradshaw) / "I've Been Around" (Glover-Theard). John "Shorty" Haughton (tb), Pritchard

Chessman (ts), Bill Davis (p), Les Erskine (g), Curly Russell (b), Tiny Bradshaw (vcl) + James Manilus, Bernard Glover (unknown instr.). New York, March 11, 1947. Savoy 650, 78 RPM record.

Tiny Bradshaw and His Orchestra, "Gravy Train" (Bernard) / "Teardrops" (Davis-Biggs-Childs-Rhodes). Leslie Ayres (tp), Rufus Gore (ts), Orrington Hall (bar, as), Jimmy Robinson (p), Leroy Harris (g), Clarence Mack (b), Calvin Shields (d), Tiny Bradshaw (vcl), unknown male vcl. Cincinnati, November 30, 1949. King 4337. 78 RPM record.

Tiny Bradshaw and His Orchestra, "Bradshaw Boogie" (Mann, Glover) / "Walkin' the Chalk Line" (Bernard, Norman). (A) Leslie Ayres (tp), Orrington Hall (as, bar), Red Prysock (ts), Jimmy Robinson (p, org), Willie Gaddy (g), Eddie Smith (b), Calvin Shields (d), Tiny Bradshaw (vcl). New York, January 16, 1951. (B) Leslie Ayres (tp), Rufus Gore (ts), Orrington Hall (bar, as), Jimmy Robinson (p), Leroy Harris (g), Clarence Mack (b), Calvin Shields (d), Tiny Bradshaw (vcl). Cincinnati, February 8, 1950. King 4457. 78 RPM record.

Tiny Bradshaw and His Orchestra, "Soft" (Bradshaw) / "Strange" (Bradshaw-Glover). Lester Bass (tp), Andrew Penn (tb), Red Prysock, Rufus Gore (ts), Jimmy Robinson (p), Clarence Mack (b), Philip Paul (d), Tiny Bradshaw (vcl). Cincinnati, October 6, 1952. King 4577. 78 RPM record.

The Tiny Grimes Swingtet, "Flying Home, Parts 1 and 2" (Goodman, Hampton). Trummy Young (tb), John Hardee (ts), Marlowe Morris (p), Tiny Grimes (g), Jimmy Butts (b), Eddie Nicholson (d). New York, August 14, 1946. Blue Note 524, 78 RPM record.

Tiny Grimes and His Rockin' Highlanders, "Battle of the Mass." Benny Golson (ts), Red Prysock (ts), poss. Freddie Redd (p), Tiny Grimes (g), Ike Isaacs (b), unknown (d). Philadelphia, September, 1950. Released 1986, Classics 5106, CD.

Red Prysock, "Hand Clappin'" (Prysock) / "Jumbo" (Prysock). Blue Mitchell (tp), Red Prysock (ts), Clarence Wright (bar), Roland Johnson (vib), Oliver Blair (p), Raymond Kitz (g), Herb Gordy (b), Purnell Rice (d). New York, July 8, 1955. Mercury 70698, 78 and 45 RPM record.

Red Prysock and His Orchestra, "Swing Softly, Red." Emmett Berry, Taft Jordan (tp), William Wells, Donald Cole (tb), James Powell (as), Red Prysock (ts), Clarence Wright (bar), Howard Whaley (p, org), Eddie McFadden (g), Milt Hinton (b), David Francis (d), Bill Rodriguez (bgo), George Laguna (cga). New York, 1958. Mercury 20512, LP record.

Joe Morris and His Orchestra, "Bam-a-lam-a-bam" (Morris) / "Boogie Woogie Joe" (Morris). Joe Morris (tp), Johnny Griffin (ts), Bill McLemore (bar), Wilmus Reeves (p), unknown, g, b, and d. New York, 1947. Manor 1128, 78 RPM record.

Joe Morris and His Orchestra, "Low Groovin'" (Morris) / "Jump with Me" (Morris). Joe Morris (tp), Johnny Griffin (ts), Bill McLemore (bar), Wilmus Reeves (p), George Freeman (g), Embra Daylie (b), Leroy Jackson (d). New York, December 12, 1947. Atlantic 855, 78 RPM record.

Joe Morris Orchestra, "Easy Riff" (Morris) / "The Applejack" (McLemore). (A) Joe Morris (tp), Johnny Griffin (ts), Bill McLemore (bar), Wilmus Reeves (p), George Freeman (g), Embra Daylie (b), Leroy Jackson (d). New York, December 12, 1947. (B) Joe Morris (tp, vcl), Matthew Gee (tb), Johnny Griffin (ts), Bill McLemore (bar), Elmo Hope (p), Percy Heath (b), Philly Joe Jones (d). New York, September 19, 1948. Atlantic 866, 78 RPM record.

Joe Morris Orchestra, "Anytime, Anyplace, Anywhere" (Morris, Tate) / "Come Back, Daddy Daddy" (Ahbert, Morris). Joe Morris (tp), unknown (tp), (as), 2 unknown (ts), Elmo Hope (p), Roy Gaines (g), unknown b and d, Laurie Tate (vcl). New York, June, 1950. Atlantic 914, 78 RPM record.

Faye Adams with the Joe Morris Orchestra, "Shake a Hand" (Morris) / "I'll Be True" (McLemore). Joe Morris (tp) + others, Faye Adams (vcl). New York, c. June 1953. Herald 416, 78 RPM record.

Frank Culley and His Band, "The Snap" (Culley) / "Floorshow" (Anderson). Frank Culley (ts), prob. Randy Weston (p), unknown g, b, prob. Connie Kay (d). New York, January 17, 1949, Atlantic 880, 78 RPM record.

Frank "Floorshow" Culley and His Band, "Cole Slaw (Sorghum Switch)" (Stone) / "Central Avenue Breakdown" (Hampton). Frank Culley (ts), prob. Randy Weston (p), unknown g, b, prob. Connie Kay (d). New York, January 17, 1949. Atlantic 874, 78 RPM record.

Frank "Floorshow" Culley and His Band, "After Hour Session" (Culley-Wall) / "Rhumboogie Jive" (Culley-Wall). Frank Culley (ts), Harry Van Walls (p), others unknown. New York, September 19, 1949. Atlantic 888, 78 RPM record.

Tab Smith His Velvet Tenor and Orchestra, "Because of You" (Hammerstein-Wilkison) / "Dee Jay Special" (Smith). Sonny Cohn (tp), Tab Smith (as, ts, vcl), Leon Washington (ts), Laverne Dillon or Teddy Brannon (p), Wilfred Middlebrooks (b), Walter Johnson (d). Chicago, August 28, 1951. United 104, 78 RPM record.

Ruth Brown with Eddie Condon's N.B.C. Television Orchestra, "It's Raining" (Farr) / "So Long" (Harris-Morgan-Melsher). Ruth Brown (vcl) acc by Bobby Hackett (tp), Will Bradley (tb), Dick Cary (alto-hrn), Peanuts Hucko (cl, ts), Ernie Caceres (bar), Joe Bushkin (p), Eddie Condon (g), Jack Lesberg (b), Sidney Catlett (d). New York, May 25, 1949. Atlantic 879, 78 RPM record.

Eddie Condon's N.B.C. Television Orchestra, "Seems Like Old Times" (Lonbaro-Loeb) / "Time Carries On" (Condon). Bobby Hackett (tp), Will Bradley (tb), Dick Cary (alto-hrn), Peanuts Hucko (cl, ts), Ernie Caceres (bar), Joe Bushkin (p), Eddie Condon (g), Jack Lesberg (b), Sidney Catlett (d), Ruth Brown (vcl). New York, May 25, 1949, Atlantic 661, 78 RPM record.

Ruth Brown with Budd Johnson's Orchestra, "I'll Get Along, Parts 1 and 2" (Fields-Marks). Ruth Brown (vcl) acc by Harold "Shorty" Baker (tp), Tyree Glenn (tb), Vincent Bair-Bey (as), Budd Johnson (ts), Ernie Caceres (bar), Earl

Washington (p), Leonard Gaskin (b), Roy Haynes (d). New York, September 18, 1949. Atlantic 887, 78 RPM record.

Ruth Brown with Budd Johnson's Orchestra (mislabeled), "Teardrops from My Eyes" (Toombs) / "Am I Making the Same Mistake Again?" (Thomas). Ruth Brown (vcl) acc by unknown tp, as, Willis Jackson (ts), prob Haywood Henry (bar), Harry Van Walls (p), unknown g, b, and d. September, 1950. Atlantic 919, 78 RPM record.

Cootie Williams and His Orchestra, "'Gator Tail Parts 1 and 2" (Williams-Jackson). Cootie Williams (tp), Bob Merrill (tp, vcl), Rupert Cole (as), Willis Jackson (ts), Lester Fauntleroy (p), Leonard Swain (b), Gus Johnson (d). New York, March 2, 1949. Mercury 8131, 78 RPM record.

Willis Jackson and His Orchestra, "On My Own" (Cobb, Kynard) / "Dance of the Lady Bug" (Cobb, Kynard). Andrew "Fats" Ford (tp), Booty Wood (tb), Willis Jackson (ts), Ben Kynard (bar), Bill Doggett (p), Leonard Swain (b), Panama Francis (d). New York, January 16, 1950. Apollo 801, 78 RPM record.

Willis Jackson and His Orchestra, "Harlem Nocturne" (Hazen) / "Street Scene" (Newman). John H. Russell (tp), Walter "Phatz" Morris (tb), Otis Sutton (as, bar), Willis Jackson (ts), Jimmy Evans (p), Leonard Swain (b), Emmanuel Simms (d). New York, July 9, 1951. Atlantic 948, 78 RPM record.

Little Willie John, "All Around the World" (Turner) / "Don't Leave Me Dear" (John). Little Willie John (vcl) acc by Willis Jackson (ts), Champion Jack Dupree (p), Mickey Baker (g), Ivan Rolle (b), Calvin Shields (d). New York, June 27, 1955. King 4818, 78 RPM record.

CHAPTER FIVE: OPEN THE DOOR

Jack McVea and His All Stars, "Open the Door Richard!" (McVea-Clarke) / "Lonesome Blues" (Tarrant). John "Red" Kelly (tp), Jack McVea (ts), Thomas "Crow" Kahn (p), unidentified (g), Frank Clarke (b), Rabon Tarrant (d, vcl). Los Angeles, July–August, 1946. Black and White 792, 78 RPM record.

Jazz at the Philharmonic, "Lester Leaps In" (Young). J. J. Johnson (tb), Illinois Jacquet, Jack McVea (ts), Nat King Cole (p), Les Paul (g), Johnny Miller (b), Lee Young (d). Philharmonic Auditorium, Los Angeles, July 2, 1944. Disc 504, 78 RPM album (Norman Granz' Jazz at the Philharmonic, Vol, 4).

Slim Gaillard, "Santa Monica Jump" (Gaillard) / "Slim's Jam" (Gaillard). Dizzy Gillespie (tp), Charlie Parker (as), Jack McVea (ts), Dodo Marmarosa (p), Slim Gaillard (g, vcl), Tiny "Bam" Brown (b), Zutty Singleton (d). Hollywood, prob. December 17, 1945. Bel-Tone 761, 78 RPM record.

Ray Charles, "St. Pete Florida Blues." Ray Charles (vcl, p) acc by Jack McVea (ts-1), Louis Speiginer (g), or poss T-Bone Walker (g), Billy Hadnott (b), Rudy Pitts (d). Florida, c. 1951. London Records 6175, LP record.

Eddie "Cleanhead" Vinson, "Kidney Stew Blues" (Blackman, Vinson) / "Old Maid Boogie" (Vinson). John Hunt (tp), Eddie "Cleanhead" Vinson (as, vcl), Lee Pope (ts), Greely Walton (bar), Earl Van Riper (p), Leonard Swain (b), Butch Ballard (d). New York, November 18, 1948. Mercury 8028, 78 RPM record.

Eddie "Mr. Cleanhead" Vinson and His Orchestra, "Juice Head Baby" (Williams-Daylie) / "Mr. Cleanhead Steps Out" (Vinson). Ellis "Stumpy" Whitlock, John Hunt, Joe Bridgewater (tp); Leon Comegys, Rip Tarrant (tb); Eddie "Cleanhead" Vinson (as, vcl); Frank Dominguez, Ernest "Lee" Turner (as); Lee Pope, Red Carmen (ts); Greely Walton (bar); Earl Van Riper (p); Leonard Swain (b); Gus Johnson (d). New York, c. December 1945. Mercury 2031, 78 RPM record.

Eddie "Cleanhead" Vinson, "Wineola" (Glover-Greer) / "Somebody Done Stole My Cherry Red" (Mann-Bernard). Henderson Williams (tp), Eddie "Cleanhead" Vinson (as, vcl), Eddie "Lockjaw" Davis (ts), Harry Porter (cl, ts), Al Townsend (bar), Wynton Kelly (p), Franklin Skeete (b), Lee Abrams (d). Cincinnati, August 16, 1949. King 4313, 78 RPM record.

Eddie "Cleanhead" Vinson, "Lonesome Train" (Glover) / "Person to Person" (Singleton-McRae). Freeman Lee (tp), Slide Hampton (tb), Eddie "Cleanhead" Vinson (as, vcl), Charlie Rouse (ts), Walter Hiles (bar), Jo Lawson (p), John Faire (g), Carl Lee (b), Wilbert Granville T. Hogan (d). Cincinnati, July 7, 1952. King 4582, 78 RPM record.

Bull Moose Jackson and His Buffalo Bearcats, "I Love You Yes I Do" (Glover, Nix) / "Sneaky Pete" (Nix). Frank Galbreath (tp), Bull Moose Jackson (ts, vcl), other personnel unknown. New York, August 1947. King 4181. 78 RPM record.

Bull Moose Jackson and His Buffalo Bearcats, "Honey Dripper" (Liggins) / "Hold Him Joe" (Peacock-Francos-Millinder). Harold "Money" Johnson (tp), Burnie Peacock (as), Bull Moose Jackson, Sam "the Man" Taylor (ts), Sir Charles Thompson (p), Bernie Mackay (g), Beverly Peer (b), Panama Francis (d), and others. New York, c. August 1945. Queen 4100, 78 RPM record.

Bull Moose Jackson acc by Tiny Bradshaw's Band (Moose Jackson on record label), "Big Ten-Inch Record" (Welsmantel) / "I Needed You" (Raban-Delmore). Bull Moose Jackson (vcl) acc by Leslie Ayres, Lester Bass (tp), Andrew Penn (tb), Ted "Snookie" Hulbert (as, bar), Red Prysock, Rufus Gore (ts), Jimmy Robinson (p), Clarence Mack (b), Philip Paul (d). Cincinnati, October 6, 1952. King, 4580. 78 and 45 RPM records.

Hal Singer Sextet, "Corn Bread" (Singer) / "A Plug for Cliff" (Singer). Milt Larkin (tb), Hal Singer (ts) [aka Hal "Cornbread" Singer (ts)], Wynton Kelly (p), Franklin Skeete (b), Heyward Jackson (d). New York, c. June 1948. Savoy 671, 78 RPM record.

Hal Singer Sextet, "Beef Stew" (Singer) / "One for Willie" (Reig). Willie Moore (tp), Alfred "Chippy" Outcalt (tb), Hal Singer (ts), George Rhodes (p),

Walter Page (b), Bobby Donaldson (d). New York, December 10, 1948. Savoy 686, 78 RPM record.

Paul Williams and His Band, "Hastings St. Bounce" (Williams) / "Way Late" (Reig-Thomas). John Lawton (tp), Paul Williams (as, bar), Walter Cox (as, ts), T. J. Fowler (p), Hank Ivory (b), Clarence Stamps (d), Alex Thomas (vcl). Detroit, September 5, 1947. Savoy 659, 78 RPM record.

Paul Williams and His Band, "Bouncing with Benson" (Williams) / "Boogie Ride" (Williams). Same personnel. October 6, 1947. Savoy 664, 78 RPM record.

Paul Williams and His Band, "35-30" (Williams) / "Come with Me Baby" (Reig). Same personnel, Johnny Cox (vcl) added. October 6, 1947. Savoy 661, 78 RPM record.

Helen Humes acc by the Bill Doggett Octet, "Every Now and Then" (Sherman-Lewis) / "Be-Baba-Leba" (Humes). Helen Humes (vcl) acc by Ross Butler (tp), John Brown (as), Wild Bill Moore (ts), Ernest Thompson (bar), Bill Doggett (p), Elmer Warner (g), Alfred Moore (b), Chiz Harris (d). Los Angeles, June 1945. Philo/Aladdin 106. 78 RPM record.

Wild Bill Moore, "We're Gonna Rock" (Moore) / "Harlem Parade" (Moore). (A) Phil Guilbeau (tp), Paul Williams (as, bar), Wild Bill Moore (ts), J. T. Fowler (p), Herman Hopkins (b), Reetham Mallett (d). Detroit, December 18, 1947. (B) Floyd Taylor (p), replaces Fowler. Detroit, November 21, 1947. Savoy 666, 78 RPM record.

Paul Williams and His Hucklebuckers, "The Huckle-Buck" (Gibson) / "Hoppin' John" (Williams). Phil Guilbeau (tp), Paul Williams (as, bar), Sam Miller (ts), Floyd Taylor (p), Herman Hopkins (b), Reetham Mallett (d). Detroit, December 15, 1948. Savoy 983, 78 RPM record.

Big Jay McNeely and His Blue Jays, "Benson's Groove" (McNeely) / "Wild Wig" (McNeely). John Anderson (tp), John "Streamline" Ewing (tb), Big Jay McNeely (ts), Bob McNeely (bar), Jimmy O'Brien (p), Ted Shirley (b), William Streetser (d). Los Angeles, November 29, 1948. Savoy 686, 78 RPM record.

Big Jay McNeely and Band, "There Is Something on Your Mind" (McNeely) / ". . . Back . . . Shack . . . Track" (McNeely-Warner). Big Jay McNeely (ts), Bob McNeely (bar), Wendell Johnson (g), Dillard McNeely (b), Leonard "Tight" Hardiman (d), Haywood "Little Sony" Warner (vcl). Live Birdland Club, Seattle, December 1957. Swingin' 614, 45 RPM record.

Earl Bostic and His Orchestra, "Temptation" (Brown, Freed) / "Artistry by Bostic" (Bostic). Roger Jones (tp, vcl), Earl Bostic (as), Ted Barnett (ts), George Parker (p), Vernon King (b), Shep Shepherd (d). New York, prob. late 1947. Gotham 158. 78 RPM record.

Earl Bostic and His Orchestra, "Flamingo" (Anderson, Grouya) / "I'm Getting Sentimental over You" (Bassman, Washington). Gene Redd (tp, vib), Earl Bostic (as), Count Hastings (ts), Cliff Smalls (p), Rene Hall (g), Keter Betts (b), Jimmy Cobb (d), Clyde Terrell (vcl). New York, January 10 and 23, 1951. King 4475, 78 RPM record.

Earl Bostic and His Orchestra, "I Hear a Rhapsody" (Gasparre, Fragos, Baker) / "Harlem Nocturne" (Hagen). Elmon Wright, Johnny Coles (tp), Earl Bostic (as), Benny Golson (ts), Larry Bunker (vib), Stash O'Laughlin (p), Barney Kessel (g), George Tucker (b), Ralph Jones (d), Kenneth Tyler (perc). Los Angeles, April 23, 1956. King 4978, 45 RPM record.

Earl Bostic and His Orchestra, "Up There in Orbit, Parts 1 and 2" (Bostic-Bass-Gray). Claude Jones (p, org), John Gray, Allan Seltzer (g), Johnny Pate (b), Redd Holt (d), Frank Rullo (perc). Chicago, October 10, 1958. King 5190, 45 RPM record.

CHAPTER SIX: DOWN IN NEW ORLEANS

Annie Laurie with Paul Gayten and His Trio, "Since I Fell for You" (Johnson) / "Love That Man of Mine" (Gayten). Annie Laurie (vcl) acc by Paul Gayten (p), Jack Scott (g), George Pryor (b), Robert Green (d). New Orleans, 1947. DeLuxe 1082, 78 RPM record.

Paul Gayten, "True" (Albert-Cottrell) / "Your Hands Ain't Clean" (Gayten). Personnel unavailable. Release date 1947. Deluxe 1063, 78 RPM record.

Dave Bartholomew and His Sextette, "Stardust" (Carmichael) / "She's Got Great Big Eyes" (Bartholomew). Dave Bartholomew (tp, vcl), Joe Harris (as), Clarence Hall (ts), Fred Lane (p), Frank Fields (b), Earl Palmer (d). New Orleans, 1947. DeLuxe 1104, 78 RPM record.

Dave Bartholomew and His Sextette, "Dave's Boogie Woogie" (Bartholomew) / "Bum Mae" (Bartholomew). Same personnel and date. DeLuxe 1114, 78 RPM record.

Dave Bartholomew, "Country Boy" / "Mr. Fool." Same personnel with Ernest McLean (g) added. New Orleans, 1949. DeLuxe 3223, 78 RPM record.

Fats Domino, "Detroit City Blues" (Bartholomew, Domino) / "The Fat Man" (Bartholomew, Domino). Personnel unavailable. New Orleans, release date 1949. Imperial 5058, 78 RPM record.

Lee Allen, "The Eel" / "Creole Alley." Joshua "Jack" Willis (tp), Waldren "Frog" Joseph (tb), Lee Allen (ts), Edward Frank (p), Justin Adams (g), Frank Fields (b), Earl Palmer (d), Earl Williams (vcl). New Orleans, June 14, 1954. Savoy SJL2234, LP record.

Roy Montrell and His Orchestra, "(Every Time I Hear) That Mellow Saxophone" (Marascalco-Montrell-Sandy) / "Oooh-Wow" (Montrell-Sandy). Roy Montrell (g, vcl) acc by Lee Allen (ts), Alvin "Red" Tyler (ts, bar), Edward Frank (p), Frank Fields (b), Earl Palmer (d). New Orleans, 1955. Specialty 583, 45 RPM record.

Lee Allen and His Band, "Rockin' at Cosmo's" (Allen) / "Shimmy" (Allen). Lee
Allen (ts), Edward Frank (p), Justin Adams (g), Frank Fields (b), Earl Palmer
(d). New Orleans, August 1956. Aladdin 3334, 45 RPM record.

Lee Allen and His Band, "Walkin' with Mr. Lee" (Allen) / "Promenade" (Tyler-
Frank). Lee Allen (ts), Allen Toussaint (org), Edward Frank (p), Edgar
Blanchard (bj), Justin Adams (g), Frank Fields (b), Charles Williams (d).
New Orleans, 1957. Ember 1027, 45 RPM record.

Lee Allen and His Band, "Cat Walk" (Allen-Toussaint) / "Creole Alley" (Allen).
Lee Allen (ts), Alvin "Red" Tyler (ts, bar), Allen Toussaint (p), Mac "Dr.
John" Rebennack (g), Frank Fields (b), Charles "Hungry" Williams (d).
New Orleans, 1959. Ember 1057, 45 RPM record.

Big Joe Turner, *Life Ain't Easy*. Big Joe Turner (vcl) acc by Roy Eldridge (tp), Al
Grey (tb), Lee Allen (ts), Jimmy Robins (p, org), Thomas Gadson (g), Ray
Brown (b), Earl Palmer (d). Los Angeles, June 3, 1974. Pablo 2310. LP record.

Fats Domino, "Blue Monday" (Bartholomew-Domino) / "What's the Reason I'm
Not Pleasing You" (Hatch, Tomlin, Poe, and Grier). Fats Domino (p, vcl),
Herb Hardesty (ts, bar), other personnel unknown. New Orleans, 1956.
Imperial 5417, 45 RPM record.

Herb Hardesty, "Perdido Street" (Reichner-Hardesty) / "Adam and Eva" (Reich-
ner-Hardesty). Herb Hardesty (ts), Clarence Ford (bar, ts), Hank Jones (p),
Roy Montrell (g), Jimmy Davis (b), Cornelius Coleman (d). New York, late
March or early April 1959. Federal 12423, 45 RPM record.

Tom Waits, "Romeo Is Bleeding" (Waits). Herb Hardesty, Frank Vicari (ts); Tom
Waits (p, g, vcl); Dawilli Gonga (keyboards); Charles Kynard (org); Harold
Battiste (p); Ray Crawford, Roland Bautista, Shine Robinson (g); Byron
Miller, Jim Hughart, Scott Edwards (b); Ricky Lawson, Alan Chip White,
Earl Palmer (d); Bobbye Porter Hall (cga). Hollywood, 1978. Asylum 53088,
LP record (*Blue Valentine*).

Red Tyler and the Gyros, "Peanut Vendor" (Simons). Alvin "Red" Tyler (ts, bar)
acc by unknown hrns, p, g, b, and d. New Orleans, late 1959/early 1960.
Ace 1006, LP record (*Rockin' and Rollin'*).

Alvin "Red" Tyler, "Lush Life" (Strayhorn). Clyde Kerr Jr. (tp), Alvin "Red" Tyler
(ts, tamb), David Torkanowsky (p), James Singleton (b), Johnny Vidacovich
(d), Johnny Adams, Germaine Bazzle (vcl). Slidell, Los Angeles, April 1985.
Rounder 2047, LP record (*Heritage*).

CHAPTER SEVEN: ROCK AND ROLL

Duke Ellington and His Orchestra, "Happy-Go-Lucky Local, Parts 1 and 2"
(Ellington). Shelton Hemphill, Taft Jordan, Cat Anderson, Harold Baker
(t); Ray Nance (t, vl, v); Lawrence Brown, Wilbur De Paris, Claude Jones

(tb); Jimmy Hamilton (cl, ts); Russell Procope (cl, as); Johnny Hodges (as); Al Sears (ts); Harry Carney (cl, as, bar); Duke Ellington (p); Fred Guy (g); Oscar Pettiford (sb); Sonny Greer (d, ch); Al Hibbler, Kay Davis, Marion Cox (v). Concert, Civic Opera House, Chicago, November 10, 1946. Musicraft 461, 78 RPM record.

Johnny Hodges and Orchestra, "That's the Blues Old Man" (Hodges-Mills) / "Queen Bess" (Hodges-Mills). Cootie Williams (tp), Lawrence Brown (tb), Johnny Hodges (sop, as), Harry Carney (bar), Duke Ellington (p), Jimmy Blanton (b), Sonny Greer (d). Chicago, November 2, 1940. Bluebird 11117, 78 RPM record.

Jimmy Forest (*sic*), "Bolo Blues" (Forrest) / "Night Train" (Forrest). Jimmy Forrest (ts), Bunky Parker (p), John Mixon (b), Oscar Oldham (d), Percy James (cga, bgo). Chicago, November 27, 1951. United 110, 78 RPM record.

Miles Davis with Jimmy Forrest Quartet/Quintet: Miles Davis (tp), Jimmy Forrest (ts, vcl), Charles Fox (p), John Mixon (b), Oscar Oldham (d), unknown (cga). The Barrel, St. Louis, spring 1952. Prestige 7860, LP record (*Live at the Barrel*).

Eddie "Lockjaw" Davis, "Huckle Boogie" (Glover) / "Mountain Oysters" (Bernard). Eddie "Lockjaw" Davis (ts), Bill Doggett (org), John Simmons (b), Jo Jones (d) + unknown tp, prob second ts, bar, b, and d + male singer. New York, August 16, 1949. King 4321, 78 RPM record.

Ella Fitzgerald, "Crying in the Chapel" (Glenn) / "When the Hands of the Clock Pray at Midnight" (Curtis). Ella Fitzgerald (vcl) acc by Taft Jordan (tp), Bill Doggett (org), Sandy Block (b), Jimmy Crawford (d), Ray Charles Singers (vcl group). New York, June 11, 1953. Decca 28762, 78 RPM record.

Bill Doggett, "Honky Tonk, Parts 1 and 2" (Doggett-Shepherd-Scott-Butler). Clifford Scott (as, ts-1), Bill Doggett (org), Billy Butler (g), Carl Pruitt (b), Shep Shepherd (d). New York, June 16, 1956. King 4950, 45 RPM record.

Doc Bagby, "Dumplin's" (Bagby) / "Sylvia's Callin'" (Baker-Bagby). Ellsworth Gooding (ts), Doc Bagby (org), Mickey Baker (g), Milt Hinton (b), Gus Johnson (d). New York, January 29, 1957. Okeh 7089, 45 RPM record.

Ray Charles, "What'd I Say? Parts 1 and 2." Ray Charles (vcl, p) acc by David "Fathead" Newman (as, ts), Hank Crawford (bar), Edgar Willis (b), Milt Turner (d) + others. New York, February 18, 1959. Atlantic 2031, 45 RPM record.

Sil Austin, "Slow Walk" (Austin) / "Wildwood" (Austin). Austin (ts, vcl), Doc Bagby (org), Ace Harris (p), Mickey Baker (g), Clarence Collier (b), Freddie Bonita (d). New York, September 4, 1956. Mercury 70963, 45 RPM record.

Noble "Thin Man" Watts and His Rhythm Sparks, "Hard Times (The Slop)" (Watts) / "I'm Walking the Floor over You" (Tubb). Noble "Thin Man" Watts (ts), Royal Hamilton (p), Jimmy Spruill, Louis Candy (g), Willie "Saint" Jenkins (d). New York, c. October 1957. Baton 249, 45 RPM record.

The Chords, "Cross over the Bridge" (Benjamin, Weiss) / "Sh-Boom" (Feasler, McRae, Keyes, Edwards). The Chords (vcl), Sam "the Man" Taylor (ts), others unknown. New York, 1954. Cat 104, 78 and 45 RPM record.

Langston Hughes with Red Allen Group. Langston Hughes (reading) acc by Henry "Red" Allen (tp), Vic Dickenson (tb), Sam "the Man" Taylor (ts), Al Williams (p), Milt Hinton (b), Osie Johnson (d). New York, March 17, 1958. MGM 3697, LP record (*The Weary Blues*).

Frankie Lymon and the Teenagers, "Why Do Fools Fall in Love?" (Lymon-Goldner)* / "Please Be Mine" (Lymon-Goldner). Frankie Lymon and group (vcl), Jimmy Wright (ts), Jimmy Shirley (g), Al Hall (b), Gene Brooks (d). New York, 1955. Gee 1002, 78 and 45 RPM record.

Hot Lips Page and group, "Sweet Georgia Brown" (Bernie, Pinkard, Casey). Hot Lips Page, Joe Guy (tp), Jimmy Wright (ts), Thelonious Monk (p), unknown (b), poss. Kenny Clarke (d). Live Minton's, New York, 1941. Onyx 207, CD.

Gone All Stars, "7-11 (Mambo No. 5)" (Prado, arranged by Goldner) / "Down Yonder Rock" (Goldner). Buddy Lucas (ts) unknown others. New York, 1957. Gone 5016, 45 RPM record.

King Curtis and His Royal Men, "Birth of the Blues" (DeSylva-Brown-Henderson) / "Jest Smoochin'" (Baker-Curtis). King Curtis (ts), Herman Foster (p), Ram Ramirez (org), Mickey Baker (g), Bob Bushnell (el-b), Jimmy Lewis (b), Belton Evans (d), Walter Spriggs (bgo). New York, February 5, 1958. Atco 6114, 45 RPM record.

The Coasters, "Yakety Yak" (Leiber-Stoller) / "Zing Went the Strings of My Heart" (Hanley). King Curtis (ts); Adolph Jacobs (g); unknown (b, d); Carl Gardner, lead tenor vocal; Cornelius "Cornell" Gunter, tenor vocal; Billy Guy, baritone vocal; Will "Dub" Jones, bass vocal. New York, March 17, 1958. Atco 6116, 45 RPM record.

CHAPTER EIGHT: JAZZ WITH A BEAT

King Curtis Quintet. Nat Adderley (tp), King Curtis (ts), Wynton Kelly (p), Paul Chambers (b), Oliver Jackson (d). Van Gelder Studio, Englewood Cliffs, NJ, April 21, 1960. New Jazz LP (*The New Scene of King Curtis*).

---

*It's a safe bet the arrangement and composer credits really belong with Buddy Lucas. George Goldner was the president of Gee Records. When the label was sold to Roulette Records, the writing credit for *Why Do Fools Fall in Love?* was changed to Lymon-Levy, for Mo Levy, the president of Roulette Records. In 1996, after a lawsuit, credit was given to Jimmy Merchant and Herman Santiago, who actually wrote the song, but that decision was overturned because Merchant and Santiago's filing of the suit fell outside the statute of limitations.

Soul Battle. Oliver Nelson, King Curtis, Jimmy Forrest (ts); Gene Casey (p); George Duvivier (b); Roy Haynes (d). Van Gelder Studio, Englewood Cliffs, New Jersey, September 9, 1960. Prestige 7223, LP record.

King Curtis, *Old Gold*. King Curtis (ts, as), Jack McDuff (o), Billy Butler, Eric Gale (g), Bob Bushnell (b), Ray Lucas (d), Willie Rodriguez (bgo, cga). Van Gelder Studio, Englewood Cliffs, New Jersey, September 19, 1961. Tru-Sound 15006, LP record.

Eddie "Lockjaw" Davis, *Jazz with a Beat*. Eddie "Lockjaw" Davis (ts), Shirley Scott (o), Carl Pruitt (b), Charlie Rice (d), Ray Barretto (cga). New York, July 16, 1956–February 5, 1957. King 566, LP record.

Jimmy Smith, *A New Sound . . . A New Star . . .* Jimmy Smith (org), Thornell Schwartz (g), Bazeley Perry (d). Van Gelder Studio, Hackensack, New Jersey, February 18, 1956. Blue Note 1512, LP record. "High And Mighty" / "You Get 'Cha," Blue Note 1635, "Midnight Sun." / "The Preacher" 1636, "Tenderly" / "Joy" 1637, 45 RPM records.

Eddie "Lockjaw" Davis, *Count Basie Presents the Eddie Davis Trio + Joe Newman*. Joe Newman (tp), Eddie "Lockjaw" Davis (ts), Shirley Scott (org), Count Basie (p), George Duvivier (b), Butch Ballard (d). New York, December 17, 18, and 19, 1957. Roulette 52007, LP record.

Index